on track ...

Judas Priest

every album, every song
from ***Rocka Rolla***
to ***Painkiller***

John Tucker

Sonicbond Publishing Limited
www.sonicbondpublishing.co.uk
Email: info@sonicbondpublishing.co.uk

First Published in the United Kingdom 2019
First Published in the United States 2019
This edition 2025

British Library Cataloguing in Publication Data:
A Catalogue record for this book is available from the British Library

ISBN 978-1-78952-531-1

Typset in ITC Garamond & Berthold Akzidenz Grotesk
Printed and bound in England

Graphic design and typesetting: Full Moon Media

on track ...

Judas Priest

every album, every song
from ***Rocka Rolla***
to ***Painkiller***

John Tucker

SONICBOND

sonicbondpublishing.com

Would you like to write for Sonicbond Publishing?

At Sonicbond Publishing we are always on the look-out for authors, particularly for our two main series:

On Track. Mixing fact with in depth analysis, the On Track series examines the work of a particular musical artist or group. All genres are considered from easy listening and jazz to 60s soul to 90s pop, via rock and metal.

On Screen. This series looks at the world of film and television. Subjects considered include directors, actors and writers, as well as entire television and film series. As with the On Track series, we balance fact with analysis.

While professional writing experience would, of course, be an advantage the most important qualification is to have real enthusiasm and knowledge of your subject. First-time authors are welcomed, but the ability to write well in English is essential.

Sonicbond Publishing has distribution throughout Europe and North America, and all books are also published in E-book form. Authors will be paid a royalty based on sales of their book.

Further details are available from www.sonicbondpublishing.co.uk. To contact us, complete the contact form there or email info@sonicbondpublishing.co.uk

on track ...
Judas Priest

Contents

Credits And Acknowledgements

Writing a book is a collaborative effort. OK, it's my job to pound the keys into submission, but many people have provided assistance in one way or another, and I'd like to thank them for their contributions. Firstly, though, it's worth pointing out that the origins of this book date back to August 2013, when I was asked to produce a book on Judas Priest for Independent Music Press's *Early Years* series. This book was duly completed, although IMP sold out to another publisher before it could be published and since then it's lain, unloved and forlorn, on my hard drive.

So the first person to thank is Stephen Lambe at Sonicbond, who was sufficiently interested in the book to greenlight a new version for the *On Track...* series. The original manuscript had to be wholly reworked – or, in music parlance, remixed and remastered – for its 2019 appearance, and a number of people's contributions to the original version have now been edited out as they just didn't fit the new format. However, their efforts the first time around are greatly appreciated, so, whether their words made the cut or not, I'd sincerely like to thank, in alphabetical order, Al Atkins, Ann Boleyn, Paul Britton, Per Brodesson, Biff Byford, Terry Dark, Phil Denton, John Gallagher, Miles Goodman, Olle Hedenström, Götz Kühnemund, Adam Lindmark, Lips, Mal Pearson, Doro Pesch, Rock 'n' Rolf, Jim Sieroto, Brian Tatler, Russ Tippins, Chris Tsangarides (R.I.P.), Willem Verbuyst and Russ Weaver. I'd also like to extend a grateful thank you to K.K. Downing, who took time out of his promotional schedule for his own autobiography to talk to me. Acknowledgement must also be due to both Geoff Barton and Steve Gett who championed Judas Priest in their respective publications *Sounds* and *Melody Maker* in the past and to Neil Daniels and Martin Popoff who have researched and recounted the band's history in their own in-depth publications.

As ever, I am indebted to some good friends for delivering the goods. There's the Lone Rangers Steve Mortimore and Keith Shapland (forever riding to the rescue with live cassettes from age-old trading circuits and cuttings and memorabilia, respectively), Ant Jones who managed to track down the drubbing given to *Killing Machine* in *Sounds* for me (a piece I've been dying to read for years), Matthias Mader for his inspiration and assistance with a number of interviews he's carried out for German publication *Rock Hard* and Olly Hahn at SPV for the images.

And, of course, no list of credits and acknowledgements is complete without thanking Lia for thirty-six years of support, guidance and proof-reading and, well, just about everything really.

By the way, please note that I've used the usual convention of writing interviews I've undertaken in the present tense, while quotes from other sources are written in the past tense. The exception to this rule is Chris Tsangarides whom I interviewed in 2013 but who sadly died in January 2018. Please also note that in the introduction to each album I've taken the credits from the original LP releases which do tend to vary from the later re-issues.

John Tucker, April 2019

Introduction – The Ballad Of Judas Priest

By the time they came to record their first album in 1974 Judas Priest – the band as they're known today – had been a recognisable unit for no more than a few months, even though their origins date back to the end of the Sixties.

The Judas Priest story really starts with a frontman called Allan – better known as Al – Atkins, who by that time was already a veteran of the local music scene in West Bromwich. Born in October 1947 Atkins had already been in a number of acts and in 1969, having left The Jug Blues Band to join Evolution and then fallen out with them, was keen to get a new outfit together. His first recruit was former Jug Blues bassist Brian 'Bruno' Stapenhill. 'I don't know why he stood by me through the years,' Atkins recalled in his autobiography Dawn Of The Metal Gods. 'His loyalty showed no bounds. I felt I had let him down badly by walking out on him and The Jug Blues Band after we had worked so hard together, but he forgave me and we both set about forming another band.' The roll call was completed by 'the best musicians from our old line-ups: Johnny Perry [guitar] from The Jug Blues Band and John Partridge on drums from Sugar Stack. It was kind of like a mini super group. It was a great idea, and for the first time in a few years, I was really excited about being in a new band. We'd all been around the block as it were, and so we shared similar ideas.'

Life, however, has a knack of springing horrible surprises. Before the band had even chosen a name for themselves, Perry was killed when the van he was driving downhill at high speed careered into a phone box. After a time the remaining members decided to continue and in September 1969 auditions were held for a new guitarist. 'After the death of John Perry – they said it was suicide; a terrible waste as I thought he had such a great future ahead of him – we eventually decided to carry on with the then-unnamed band,' recalls Atkins now. 'One of the guitarists that came to the audition was a local seventeen-year-old lad called Kenneth Downing. The bass player Bruno and myself held the audition and we decided the best way was to jam out a twelve bar with Bruno to see how good the players could improvise and show their skills. Kenneth plugged his guitar into his wah-wah pedal and gave it his best shot, but we couldn't really tell what he was trying to do so we passed on him.' With Downing's inexperience being his stumbling block when his slot ended he was politely asked to close the door on his way out. 'Another young lad by the name of Ernie Chataway from Birmingham was far better, and he could also play keyboards, so we gave him the job. Kenneth left a lasting impression on me though, that's true, but it was more through his good looks and a long mane of naturally blonde hair. There's no doubt that he would've certainly pulled the young groupies!'

So now there was a band once more, albeit one without a name to put on their gig posters. Collectively Atkins, Chataway, Stapenhill and Partridge were impressed by another local act called Black Sabbath. 'Ernie, our new guitarist, had been with the same Birmingham agency as a band called Earth but they had now changed their name to Black Sabbath,' says Atkins. 'We all thought that was a wicked name so we decided to find a similar double-barrelled, sinister title that would grab people's attention, and it was Bruno who came up with Judas Priest.' Stapenhill, it appears, was a bit of a Bob Dylan fan, and on the album John Wesley Harding he came across 'The Ballad Of Frankie Lee and Judas Priest'. Suggesting the idea Judas Priest to his bandmates a couple of days later, the bassist unwittingly sowed the seeds for the birth of a legend.

A demo tape featuring 'Good Time Woman' and 'We'll Stay Together', and numerous successful gigs (which later included a well-intentioned but seemingly disastrous tour of Scotland) led to a contract with the aptly-named London-based Immediate Records – aptly-named because they immediately went bust. Despite this early momentum Judas Priest began to drift. The band played their last gig in April 1970 and split amicably a short while later. 'Immediate Records going bust was a real kick in the teeth,' says Atkins, 'so that didn't help our motivation at all. But I wanted to go down the same road as Sabbath with a heavier approach to the music. Ernie was a great player but was more a blues-style player (and still is, come to that), Bruno was offered a job playing in Denmark and I really wasn't very happy with the drummer's commitment, so it wasn't just one thing that made us split up; there were a number of reasons really. We still keep in touch, so there were no hard feelings about it.' Another band – The Bakerloo Blues Band – came and went and by October 1970 Atkins was considering putting a new 'musicians' wanted' ad in the paper. But first, on a whim, he paid a visit to Holy Joe's.

A former school a few miles outside of West Bromwich, Holy Joe's (as it was nicknamed by those who used it) had been turned into rehearsal rooms and was a good place to spot up-and-coming acts. That particular night his interest was piqued by the sound of a band going through its paces, and Atkins quickly recognised the guitarist as a now more experienced Ken Downing. 'When they finished their song I knocked and popped my head round to see Kenny with his new band called Freight. They were a power trio with Ian Hill on bass and John Ellis on drums. My first thought was that Kenny's guitar playing had got a lot better since those auditions we did a year earlier, but he still liked his wah pedal a bit too much – Kenny was always a massive Jimi Hendrix fan! Anyway, I told them I was looking for a band and asked if they'd be interested in me fronting them and they all agreed, but I didn't like the name Freight at all so suggested my old band's name, and so Judas Priest 2 was born. Just talking to them for the first time I could feel their enthusiasm; they were all around eighteen years old or so, and they were young and hungry for it. They were just what I was looking for.'

The Freight lads realised that if they took up Atkins' suggestion of using the Judas Priest moniker they could trade on the reputation that the band had built up locally and perhaps at least start from square two rather than square one. The quartet began rehearsing solidly, and as 1971 dawned the name, Judas Priest was starting to appear on flyers and gig posters once more. The Atkins / Downing / Hill / Ellis line-up made its live debut on 16 March 1971.

Early gigs – as ever in such situations – contained a smattering of originals amongst a set of covers, with early versions of the likes of 'Never Satisfied', 'Winter' and 'Caviar And Meths' starting to make themselves known to small but enthusiastic audiences. Much later, at the time of February 1973's Heavy Thoughts tour the setlist was: 'Spanish Castle Magic' / 'Winter' / 'Voodoo Rag' / 'Never Satisfied' / 'Joey' / 'Whiskey Woman' / 'Mind Conception' / 'Black Sheep Of The Family' / 'Holy Is The Man' / 'Caviar And Meths'; according to Atkins' autobiography. 'Spanish Castle Magic' was included in the set, naturally, as Downing's homage to his idol.

By July 1971 the band were in good enough shape to record a demo, and a trip to Zella Studios in Birmingham resulted in two Atkins' compositions 'Holy Is the Man' and 'Mind Conception' being put to tape. But before the band went much further Ellis quit on 6 October, announcing at a gig with Slade that he was leaving that night. (Interestingly, by default Judas Priest 'headlined' the show because Slade had another gig to do so had to get on stage, get down and get with it, and get back in the van and drive to the next venue as quickly as possible.) His replacement, Alan Moore, was found via an advert in a music shop window, but his tenure wasn't to last long as a band called Sundance made him a better offer, so he upped sticks and left. Next behind the drum kit came Jamaican Chris 'Congo' Campbell, 'more photogenic than our previous drummers,' notes Atkins, 'a young, strong-looking black lad with a big Afro, which was obviously a complete contrast to Kenny's blond mane.' Once again, the band began to slog around the local gig circuit, spending more than they earned, and for Atkins, the reality of supporting a wife and child finally caught up with him. In April 1973 after the Heavy Thoughts tour, Atkins quit, and Judas Priest disbanded again. Kind of…

Younger and with no dependents, Downing and Hill were keen to keep plugging away, and a new line-up made its debut at Bolton Town Hall on 17 July 1973. Behind the drum kit sat John Hinch and, up front and centre, stood Robert John Arthur Halford, whose sister Sue Ian Hill was dating at the time. As Halford told Steve Gett in *Judas Priest – Heavy Duty*: 'One night, Sue told me that the job was up for grabs and asked if I might be interested. So I went over to K.K. and Ian's place, which was an apartment just outside Birmingham and I sat in the bedroom with them for a couple of hours talking about music and different things. Since they were also checking out drummers, I suggested bringing in John Hinch who had been in my previous band Hiroshima. All four of us then went up to Holy Joe's for an all-night rehearsal, and everything just seemed to click. They liked my voice and John's drumming and told us that the jobs were ours if we wanted them.' Hearing Halford – a man with one of the most powerful voices in metal and a distinctive four-plus octave range – singing along to a Doris Day record, and his ability to play the harmonica (harmonicas, like hats, were an essential part of any early Seventies rock band) apparently also helped. Thanks to the band's manager-cum-general factotum, Dave 'Corky' Corke, Priest's latest demo featuring 'Caviar And Meths', 'Ladies', and 'Run Of

The Mill' ended up on David Howell's desk at Gull Records, and he popped along to see the band both at London's Marquee and at the Fulham Greyhound in February 1974.

Before they got that far though, they still had to sort out the name, which technically belonged to Atkins. Downing and Hill visited their former singer and popped the question. Despite feeling that 'deep down I knew I wanted to reform Judas Priest again,' he noted in his autobiography, 'I wasn't prepared to put more work into a band that produced pennies and played small clubs.' He blessed the pair with the name, and also the lyrics to the band's live material.

'You have to remember,' the singer says now, 'that we were together from 1970 to May 1973 and we'd all worked very hard over that time, clawing our way up from the small clubs to the bigger venues playing alongside Thin Lizzy, Slade, Status Quo, Budgie and Black Sabbath to name a few. We played over 150 gigs in 1972 so it was not hard for me to give up the name and my songs to them after I left because I felt they deserved it.'

Aside from royalties from the handful of Atkins-penned songs Judas Priest would record, he and the band severed all ties at that point. For a number of years the frontman who once said 'OK, we'll give it a go; it's better than other names we've had anyway' when Stapenhill had suggested calling the band Judas Priest was effectively airbrushed out of the picture.

The new-look Judas Priest spent a lot of the second half of 1973 establishing themselves and writing new material, and 1974 opened with a string of UK dates followed by their first overseas tour, a freezing cold slog through Germany and the Netherlands from 19 February to 4 March. Back in the UK another couple of weeks of domestic dates followed before Halford, Downing, Hill and Hinch dug out their passports once more and set off for a tour of Scandinavia which kept them busy from 25 March to 7 April; and it was sometime during the tour that they found out that Gull Records were keen to offer them a contract. Travelling to London on 16 April, the four members of Judas Priest signed on the dotted line.

There was, however, one small sticking point. According to Howells, he wanted the band to recruit a second guitarist. 'At MCA I'd worked with Wishbone Ash,' he told Neil Daniels, in his *The Story Of Judas Priest – Defenders Of The Faith*, 'and it seemed to me that the adoption of their twin guitar signature to Judas Priest's heavier, fatter sound would beautifully underpin Rob's extraordinary voice.' In his autobiography, Downing recalls it differently, claiming that Howells had suggested a saxophonist or a keyboard player before the proposition of a second guitarist came up. 'The record company said they would record the band, but really they would prefer [another member], they said, because of the four-piece line-up… They said there's so many other bands out there – Zeppelin, Sabbath, Stray – all with the same line-up, so could we make it a bit different. Sax player? Fuck off,' Downing laughs now. 'Not doing that, you know!

'But when I thought about it, I thought another guitar player really is an option, because a two-guitar band – a heavy two-guitar band – didn't really exist. All the harmony-type bands were lightweight. Even Wishbone Ash, who I wasn't a big fan of but I was aware of, weren't doing what I had in mind. But another guitar player in a heavy band, I could see that working. We could do harmonies, but we'd make them heavy harmonies, which is hard to do; when you harmonise, it's supposed to sound all sweet and melodic. But we did manage to do that. And then, obviously, when I would solo on stage there would still be a rhythm player there and vice-versa, and we could create that stereo guitar effect on stage and on record. So I started thinking, yeah, two lead players – could be great. And Glenn's band had just folded, so he became available.'

The final member of the Judas Priest jigsaw came from the wreckage of the now-defunct and unfeasibly-named The Flying Hat Band, a trio well-known around the Midlands. Featuring Glenn Tipton, bassist Peter 'Mars' Cowling and drummer Steve Palmer, their biggest claim to fame was supporting Deep Purple on the band's five nights in Europe in January 1974 where Purple continued to road-test their new set (and new line-up) based around the Burn album, before heading off to America (although the US tour this was supposed to lead into had to be postponed when Jon Lord went down with appendicitis). Tipton threw in his lot with Judas Priest; Mars Cowling would go on to join the Pat Travers Band alongside Nicko McBrain, and Steve (brother of Carl) Palmer would later turn up in the short-lived and even more unfeasibly-named Mantle Swallow Palmer, whose 'Ice Cold Diamond' contribution to Heavy Metal Heroes Vol.II is the only real recording that can be traced to him.

Incidentally, it was also thanks to Dave Corke that Ken morphed into K.K. Back when they were still a four-piece he mocked up a poster with pictures of the musicians. 'Ian's might have said something like Ian 'Skull' Hill (Ian's head had always looked like a skull, ever since secondary school.),' he noted in his autobiography. 'Then there was Rob 'The Queen' Halford. It's easy to figure out where he conjured that one up from! And finally, there was Ken 'K.K.' Downing. Seeing it in bold on the poster, I thought, 'oooh, I like that.'

Although lacking in direction, and certainly missing the point when it came to image – wearing a mixture of whatever satin and tat local boutiques had to offer – the five-piece Judas Priest were ready to take on the world. Almost.

Rocka Rolla (1974)

Personnel:
K.K. Downing: guitars
Glen [sic] Tipton: guitars, synthesisers, second vocals
Ian Hill: bass guitar
Bob Halford: vocals, harmonica
John Hinch: drums
Record label: Gull
Recorded at Olympic, Trident and Island Studios, London, June/July 1974
Produced by: Rodger Bain
Release date: 6 September 1974
Highest chart positions: did not chart
Running time: 38:49

> ***It sounded fucking awful. Although the material we were doing wasn't bad it turned out to be a terrible recording*** – Ian Hill, quoted in ***Judas Priest – Heavy Duty***

Bassist Ian Hill's description of Judas Priest's debut album is about as mortal as a self-inflicted wound can be. But is Judas Priest's first album that bad? Put in context, a substantial number of people only came to it in retrospect, once the band were becoming a household name, and if you'd just played *Killing Machine* to death, racing out to buy *Rocka Rolla* wouldn't really give the average fan much satisfaction. But it is what it is – a solid, hugely Seventies-sounding debut from a young band still in the throes of evolution. It's not particularly focussed, and the band seem to want to be every one of their peers, from Budgie (whom they'd supported quite often) to Queen at the same time.

True to their word, Gull put the new, five-piece Judas Priest into the studio – or studios, as the album was recorded across London at Olympic, Trident and Island – for three weeks in the summer of 1974. Producer Rodger Bain was David Howells' choice, having worked with him at MCA where Bain had brought Budgie's first two albums Budgie and Squawk to life. He'd also, more famously, produced those all-important first three Black Sabbath albums. Bain had been a house producer for Vertigo Records, Sabbath's first label, and when producer Gus Dudgeon refused to work on Sabbath's debut album, telling the band to come back when they could write songs and play their instruments, Bain picked up the ball and ran with it. And boy, did he run.

Rocka Rolla, however, didn't have the impact, in any shape or form, of those early Sabbath albums. Despite the fact – or perhaps because – the album was recorded with the band playing live (it was after all, like many bands of the time, their live set played in the studio) rather than being layered with drums, rhythm tracks, vocals and so on, being put to tape separately and mixed together, K.K. Downing recalls that they were more than aware that they were running out of time and seemed to be constantly working against the clock. 'It sounded great all the way along in the recording process, it sounded pretty powerful and of course, we were playing live in the studio in those days, that's the way it was done. We heard things back in the control room and it sounded great. But it was the mastering… It seemed to have the life mastered out of it somewhere really. So we were a bit disappointed with that. But I'm not going to take anything away, in any way, shape or form, from the material, and from who we were and what we were doing. But it was a tough session. We were sleeping in a van outside the studio, things like that. It was tough. That last session, it was at least thirty-six hours, nobody had any sleep, our producer Rodger, bless him, was asleep on the couch, we'd finished the last mix, and he woke up, went upstairs at seven o'clock in the morning and cut the record. You can't do that!' the guitarist complains, 'you need fresh ears. You need to have a good night's sleep and come back to it. And Rodger wasn't a cutting engineer. But irrespective of anything I'm not going to denounce the album. Chris Tsangarides remastered it later on and it sounded considerably better.'

The first fruits of these sessions came in August 1974 with the appearance of the first ever commercial release to bear the Judas Priest name, a 7" single with 'Rocka Rolla' as the A-side and 'Never Satisfied' on the flip. The album *Rocka Rolla* followed on 6 September; some sources give it an August release date though as so few people even noticed its arrival in the shops it's hard to be accurate!

'One For The Road' (K.K. Downing / B. Halford)

So, back in 1974, as the days grew shorter and summer gave way to autumn, if you hadn't heard the band's debut single or come across a live show this would be your introduction to this new band from Birmingham. Things get rolling with the direct, no-nonsense 'One For The Road', a heavy, punchy Downing/Halford composition (incidentally, the eagle-eyed will notice that the original album credits Glenn with just one 'n' and the vocalist as Bob, while Al Atkins' first name seems to be completely forgotten) with a classy groove through the verse and a time-changing chorus. A song that wouldn't really be out of place on a Nazareth album of the time, it's shot through with succinct although not particularly fluid solos.

'Rocka Rolla' (G. Tipton / K.K. Downing / B. Halford)

Much more accessible than the preceding track, 'Rocka Rolla' was the album's obvious choice for a single. It's more of a bouncy pop song, immediate and toe-tapping, and also an early indication that lyrical definition was expendable so long as there was a good rhyme to be had; and so the description of the 'Rocka Rolla woman' of the title as 'a classy, flashy, lassie' is not the finest line to be found on a Priest album. Tipton is the main soloist in the piece, with Downing providing the closing flurry and a rare solo from Halford earns him his harmonica credit on the sleeve.

'Winter' (K.K. Downing / I. Hill / Atkins) / **'Deep Freeze'** (K.K. Downing) / **'Winter Retreat'** (K.K. Downing / B. Halford) / **'Cheater'** (K.K. Downing / B.Halford)

Although listed as separate tracks on the album sleeve (yet bracketed together in terms of running time) tracks three to six on Side One are given over to the nine-minute-and-forty-second 'Winter Suite', although quite what the final track 'Cheater' has to do with it is anyone's guess.

'Winter' was originally an Al Atkins idea inspired by the Scottish tour – actually, more a catalogue of disasters – he undertook with the Chataway, Stapenhill and Partridge line-up early in 1970. Partridge had flu and, deciding he was too ill to travel, stayed home, leaving Atkins to both sing and play the drums. Roadie John 'Magnet' Ward, who'd later join the Deep Purple organisation, had broken his left arm but was happy to drive from West Bromwich so long as whoever sat in the passenger seat changed gear for him; and one of the van's door windows was jammed open, leaving the occupants at the mercy of the snow which started to fall as the van reached Cumbria. And then things got worse. Some dodgy gigs, rough crowds and Chataway's skin allergy making him look like 'the TV comedy character Mr Blobby on a bad day…' is how Atkins summarised it in his autobiography.

Because the original album doesn't specify the actual breaks, these have been left at the mercy of CD programmers inserting track spacing where they felt fit. So, the lengths of the individual tracks have seemingly been agreed at 'Winter' 1:41, 'Deep Freeze' 1:21, 'Winter Retreat' 3:28 and then 'Cheater' 2:59. But, setting 'Cheater' aside for the moment, the CD breaks don't make sense. At the point where, on CD, 'Deep Freeze' is supposed to begin a drum break merely gives rise to a continuation of 'Winter'. The CD track 'Winter Retreat' which, to be fair, does sound like a laid-back piece, begins with nearly two minutes of Downing's finest Hendrix impression; after he's finished noodling away a slower, more accomplished semi-acoustic vocal piece takes the song to its conclusion.

The actual songs are probably more 'Winter', with its grinding riff and mid-section drum break running for around two minutes fifty-eight seconds, followed by 'Deep Freeze' (Downing's solo guitar workout) clocking in at about 1:56 with the gentle 'Winter Retreat' ballad (1:30) completing the piece. Quite why the Halford/Downing song 'Cheater' was also grouped into the 'Winter Suite' is open to conjecture, although the short stomper with its ham-fisted lyrics of a man who recalls discovering his wife in bed with another man, that he 'reached the dressing table, kicked away the door / I gripped the cold black metal, a loaded .44' does have a certain charm. It features another appearance of Halford's harmonica and wraps the side up nicely.

'Never Satisfied' (K.K. Downing / Atkins)

Side Two kicks off with the slow and rumbling 'Never Satisfied'. A not particularly remarkable outing, it's an older Downing/Atkins offering which stumbles blindly along, never appearing to know what it wants to be, although it does sit firmly at the heavier end of the album. The midway solo and closing passage lift it from the mundane and take it into more progressive territory, and Halford's final line is delivered with what would become a trademark scream. The song achieved its four-minutes-and-fifty-seconds of fame when Gull re-issued it as one of three tracks (along with 'Ripper' and 'Victim Of Changes') on a 12" single in 1980 in a blatant attempt to cash in on the remarkable success of *British Steel*, and its accompanying singles.

'Run Of The Mill' (K.K. Downing / B. Halford / G. Tipton)

You can dazzle your friends with the piece of trivia that at, eight minutes and thirty seconds, 'Run Of The Mill' was the band's longest studio cut until it was topped by 'Cathedral Spires' on the 1997 *Jugulator* album. More to the point, this epic and beautifully sparse composition with its plaintive vocal delivery is worth the price of the album alone, and highlights the latent progressive side of the band which they'd showcase later with the likes of 'Victim Of Changes' and 'Beyond The Realms Of Death'. Supposedly written by Downing specifically to showcase Halford's range, the song was demoed sometime in 1973, and it was this tape that manager Dave Corke took to Gull Records. After the verses have been despatched the two guitarists are set free to enjoy themselves in almost freeform jam mode until Halford returns to the fold and turns in a stunning, spine-chilling performance to wrap things up. File under 'lost classics'.

'Dying To Meet You' (K.K. Downing / B.Halford)

'Dying To Meet You' also lifts the quotient of big-hitters with its seemingly off-kilter chorus and left-field final third: once it appears the song has finished the band crash back in with what's pretty much a completely different song (and which is reminiscent of 'Stained Class'). Unlike 'Run Of The Mill' though it rarely hits the target, despite a cracking solo in this final section, and just rambles its way through its six-and-a-quarter minute running time.

'Caviar And Meths' (K.K. Downing / I. Hill / Atkins)

Album closer 'Caviar And Meths' was an old stage favourite and, although it might appear to have delusions of grandeur here, the sub-two-minute instrumental which closes the album is but a slice of a song that would stretch out for over six times that length as the band's live finale. Coming as it does at the end of the record, it's almost as if Rodger Bain realised that the album was a bit light in terms of running time and chopped a section out of this song to pad it out.

NWOBHM act Scarab's Paul Britton is a lifelong Priest fan who notes that it took Downing and Tipton 'all of May 1974 to knock the old song version into a twin guitar arrangement, before going into the studio to record the album. History tells us not everything went to plan, and it was pretty obvious from the start of the sessions that Rodger Bain would rule the proceedings, chopping and changing songs as he saw fit, leaving a very studio-green Judas Priest to naively trust his credential-packed experience, a decision they'd regret (but ultimately learn from). When the final cut was revealed, he'd, amongst other production follies, cut the thirteen-minute epic 'Caviar And Meths' down to a pointless two or so minutes, leaving the rest of the song's eleven smouldering minutes on the studio floor, never to be heard again.'

Post Album Events

If the record's audio quality left the band feeling under-whelmed the iconic cover image of a Coke-Cola bottle top emblazoned instead with the title *Rocka Rolla* didn't endear itself to the musicians either. Despite winning several graphic design awards, the cover was either a homage or an imitation, depending on how you take it, and bore no resemblance to the kind of music that Priest were peddling: not 'the real thing' indeed. Nor was their original singer impressed. 'I had already turned down two or three independent labels when I was with them,' recalls Al Atkins, 'but oddly they jumped at the first deal offered to them by Gull Records, which surprised me. I didn't like *Rocka Rolla* or its cover, and I thought it sounded very weak; the addition of Glenn Tipton made a big difference to the band with those twin guitars but I would have liked to have heard someone like John Bonham on drums to give it some backbone; after all, John Hinch was a blues-type drummer. Their manager Dave Corke bought the album round to my house and asked my opinion of it, and I just said, "look, Dave, I've been left over a year now, and it's their call; it's nothing to do with me".'

With *Rocka Rolla* making no attempt to bother the charts whatsoever, the band could have been dead in the water there and then. However, Gull were happy to offer them another shot, and two pivotal events indicated that far from being a bunch of scuffers, this was a band with potential by the bucketload. The first was an appearance on the *Old Grey Whistle Test* in April 1975 and the second their slot at the Reading Festival a few months later in August.

The Old Grey Whistle Test was a late-night BBC TV programme, a kind of *Top Of The Pops* for consenting adults where 'serious' bands were taped going through their paces live (but without an audience) rather than miming in front of a bunch of teenyboppers. For their two songs, aired on 25 April, Judas Priest romped through 'Rocka Rolla', with a rather fey Rob Halford mugging the camera for all his worth, before unleashing the previously unheard – that's assuming that any of the people watching that night had actually heard the first album – and exceptionally powerful 'Dreamer Deceiver' / 'Deceiver'. If this was a pointer of what was to come, then surely big things were on offer.

'K.K. Downing was the reason I picked up the guitar,' acknowledges Paul Britton. 'I was a fifteen-year-old lad who'd just spent three years learning to play Cozy Powell's hit single 'Dance With The Devil' on the drums when K.K. and his 1966 Gibson SG standard appeared before my eyes. My introduction to Judas Priest came via 'Rocka Rolla' on *Old Grey Whistle Test*, footage that of course, everyone has seen now but which in 1975 was ground-breaking – as well as shockingly out of tune in parts! – for someone like me who was into Sweet and Slade. *Rocka Rolla*, for all its confused and pretty directionless Brummie swagger and bombastic theatrical sound, was the perfect preview for what was to come. So what if Halford did look a bit, well, camp? I didn't care; I loved the man, his voice, his attitude. And more importantly to me, in my opinion in Judas Priest, there was a guitar god for a new generation. I wouldn't want to take anything away from Tipton, but he played his SG under his chin, a far too serious Hank Marvin style for me; on the other side of the set though was K.K. Downing, and he just looked so cool. It was K.K., dressed like some kind of chiffon nightmare, who really had me mesmerised. He had his SG 'shooting from the hip,' slung low, and the shapes that he threw made the hairs on my neck stand up. Watching it back now is quite an odd experience: I mean, you can hear it's Priest if you shut your eyes, but you can't quite believe it!'

An 'odd experience' indeed, and one not repeated for a long time. It would be almost four years, four albums and three drummers before Judas Priest appeared on UK TV screens again. And by the time they did, they would look and sound very, very different indeed.

Following this, Judas Priest were the second band to play on the opening day of that year's Reading Festival, on 22 August, as part of a bill headlined by Hawkwind, Yes and Wishbone Ash. Despite their low billing, the band had a fifty-five minute slot which was probably the most important fifty-five minutes of their career. There was no caution in their set ('Victim Of Changes' / 'Dreamer Deceiver' / 'Deceiver' / 'Ripper' / 'Mother Sun' / 'Island Of Domination' / K.K. Downing's guitar solo / 'Rocka Rolla') and they stormed out with a full-throttle choice of material and a take-it-or-leave-it attitude.

Reviewing the opening day for the Reading Evening Post, Robin Smith noted: 'When Judas Priest appeared, things looked up. Lesson number one at a festival is to get the audience on their feet and clapping. Judas Priest have a commanding, self-assured air. Lead singer Bob Halford, resplendent in medieval style jacket, had the audience in the palm of his hand. Following in the footsteps of Black Sabbath and Budgie, Judas Priest's music is as heavy as a ton of lead. Guitarists K. K. Downing and Glenn Tipton set up a relentless assault – cutting across one another and then spiralling off individually. At one point K. K. launched off into a Hendrix style solo, sounds catapulting across from one set of speakers to the others. Strangely the rhythm section seems to be lacking in the band. Bass and drums were drowned out, as Tipton and Downing thrashed away.'

The song of most interest in the set is 'Mother Sun' – referred to occasionally as 'Mother Son' although the opening line 'Mother Sun pouring out her heart every single day' (and yes, it does sound better than it reads) clarifies the title nicely. A rather twee opening covers familiar territory to 'Dreamer Deceiver' before giving way to a mid-section Metallica would be proud of (had they existed at this time) and then becoming the younger sibling of Scorpions' 'Fly

To The Rainbow'. The song could have been given some shape in the studio, but in its infancy it's very much a child of Seventies progressive rock, and it rambles like a bunch of pensioners on a Sunday afternoon outing before remembering that it is, in fact, a Judas Priest song and getting back to the point for a heavy, climactic ending. It's a shame that, like *Rocka Rolla*, it got left behind as the band moved forward.

To this day, *Rocka Rolla* is the album that time – and the band – forgot. Tipton would later tell Steve Gett that, in his opinion, *Sad Wings Of Destiny* was 'the first proper Judas Priest album'. Whereas songs from the second album would stay in the band's live repertoire for all time, the *Rocka Rolla* material was slowly eased out, although there's evidence that the title track was still in the set on some of the US shows in 1977. Certainly by the *Stained Class* UK tour in early 1978, all vestiges of the first album had been erased, and it wasn't until the 2011/2012 Epitaph tour, when the band pledged to play at least one track off every album – every album that featured Rob Halford, that is – that 'Never Satisfied' was taken out of the wardrobe and dusted down once more.

Rocka Rolla has been repackaged a number of times over the years, possibly most famously when EMI's budget-price re-issues imprint 'Fame' made it available in 1985. To cash in on the band's later striking fantasy cover art featuring the likes of The Hellion and The Metallion, the original bottle-top illustration was ditched in favour of a warrior-cum-bomber created by Melvyn Grant which had already adorned the jacket of Michael Moorcock's 1981 novel The Steel Tsar. Striking, maybe, but about as far removed from the album's content as you could wish to imagine and a bit of a cash-in, to be honest.

A further twist on the material came in March 1998 when, years after he'd waved goodbye to the Priest name, Al Atkins released Victim Of Changes, an album which, in the main, comprised a selection of Judas Priest songs with which he was connected, including those that fell by the wayside like 'Mind Conception' and 'Holy Is The Man' and a 'short' – seven-or-so-minute – version of 'Caviar And Meths'. To cement the Priest connection further the album also featured by then ex-Judas Priest (although not yet even in this story) skinsman Dave Holland. Although pleased with the way the album turned out, his displeasure at the cover – a needless spin on the *Sin After Sin* sepulchre – is graphically described in his autobiography as 'fucking shit!'

Sad Wings Of Destiny (1976)

Personnel:
K.K. Downing: guitars
Glenn Tipton: guitars, piano
Robert Halford: vocals
Ian Hill: bass guitar
Alan Moore: drums
Record label: Gull
Recorded at Rockfield and Morgan Studios, November 1975 – January 1976
Produced by: Jeffrey Calvert, Max West [Geraint Hughes] and Judas Priest
Release date: 23 March 1976
Highest chart positions: did not chart
Running time: 39:16

> *A different producer and the return of my old drummer, Alan Moore, made a big difference and, to me,* Sad Wings Of Destiny *was the album that became the benchmark for everything else they ever did* – Al Atkins

A band's second album can be a notoriously tricky affair. The usual problem is that all the old tried and trusted songs that have been worked up over time have been used on the first album, leaving the band to come up with a whole new forty minutes of material, sometimes at short notice. Even some of the big names like, for example, Deep Purple and Iron Maiden have struggled when the time came to go back into the studio for the second time. On the other hand, some bands – Black Sabbath being one that springs to mind – came out with a follow-up that was even better than their debut; and another such band was Judas Priest. 1976's *Sad Wings Of Destiny* is many fans' favourite to this day, and at least four of its tracks have become synonymous with the band: despite being over forty years old 'Victim Of Changes', 'Ripper', 'Tyrant' and 'Genocide' remain amongst the strongest songs Priest have ever served up.

The band already had 'Tyrant', 'Epitaph', 'Ripper' and the embryonic 'Victim Of Changes' up their sleeves when they started recording *Rocka Rolla* but they failed to make the cut. Some say that Bain didn't consider them good enough. By the time they started work on their second album 'Victim Of Changes' had morphed into the song it is today, and 'Dreamer Deceiver'/ 'Deceiver' and 'Island Of Domination' were already so familiar that the band had been happy to air them at Reading.

At the time of his death in January 2018, Chris Tsangarides was a world-class producer with endless credits to his name. Back at the end of 1975 he was nineteen years old and an assistant at Morgan Studios when Judas Priest arrived to complete *Sad Wings Of Destiny*.

> *They put me on that album as an assistant, that's how I started out, and the first thing I remember is walking into the studio and seeing K.K. Downing flailing around, playing on a wah-wah pedal and his whammy*

bar going absolutely ballistic on the middle bit of what became 'Ripper'. Despite my surprise, I thought, oh, I like this. I think I'll stay! I'd had no say in it as I'd just been assigned to Judas Priest, but my luck was definitely in that day!

The backing tracks were done at Rockfield Studios in Wales. I did go up to visit them while they were there. Motörhead were in the other studio. I went and said hello to them when I pitched up – I was there for the weekend – and when I left they seemed to be in exactly the same position as I'd seen them when I'd arrived on the first day, listening to what appeared to be the same song, at a blistering volume.

From memory, the album was done in blocks. Priest would be in for a few weeks, and then they'd go off and play somewhere, and then they'd come back, and the recording seemed to stretch from around November '75 into '76. I can't remember exact dates now but it certainly went on for a few months, and in between, I'd go and see them play at whatever college they were playing at and we developed a good friendship as well.

The production credit on the album was 'Jeffrey Calvert, Max West and Judas Priest', with the humble assistant's name spelt incorrectly. Calvert and West had already tasted the big time with a novelty hit in the summer of 1975 called 'Barbados'. 'And for my sins, I did their album Barbados Sky as well,' laughed Tsangarides. 'Jeff and Geraint, or Max to give him his professional name, came up with this bloody song 'Barbados' and they demoed it up. The managing director of Morgan Studios was the director of Gull Records, and as Gull's offices were above the studio, they were pretty much the same organisation. Anyway, Gull heard it and said, 'yes, go on, make a single'. So they made a single, it was a hit, and so suddenly they were 'hit producers' and so next it was 'go in with Judas Priest'. Priest had their own ideas, however, with what they wanted to do, and Jeff and Max were sort of engineering it and letting them get on with it.

'I got promoted to engineer when Jeff was taken ill on the session. They just said, 'well, you might as well carry on,' even though I barely knew one end of a microphone from another. I'd only been there about four or five months but, okey dokey, in I jumped, and it seemed to work, so I just carried on with it.

What I liked about Judas Priest was that the music was so interesting. They liked Queen a lot, or Rob did, and I think in his head (not that I twigged this then; this came later when I'd learned a few things) that Rob wanted to be like Freddie with all the harmonies and whatnot, so we did do quite a few backing vocals. And of course, he has this almighty range from really low stuff to his high-pitched screams. And I liked that, I really just 'got' the music; even in those tender years it was right up my street, exactly where I was coming from; and I've realised that whenever I play or do something for myself, it tends to be in Priest's sort of style from that era. It was a bit progressive, I suppose, for want of a better word; not that

> *they thought they were being progressive, they were just doing what they thought they should do.*

It wouldn't be Judas Priest though if there wasn't a new drummer in tow, and the band now featured Alan Moore sat at the back once more. The 'better offer' he'd quit and joined Sundance for was, it appeared, too good to be true after all. Jon Hinch left after the Reading 1975 show, the reasons for his departure being contentious and/or shrouded in mystery. In Neil Daniels' book *Defenders Of The Faith* he makes clear he was a hard worker – van driver, general fixer, roadie as well as drummer – who cared about the band. 'Glenn came round one day, and there were a few things that had gone wrong – he was not happy, and that's when I just thought enough is enough, and they agreed and that was it, I left… and from there, I just sort of launched myself into … a normal life,' although quite how managing Sutton Coldfield's Jameson Raid amongst other things can be considered 'a normal life' is anyone's guess. But having been an integral part of working up the bulk of the material for *Sad Wings Of Destiny* Hinch was disappointed at not even getting a mention on the album sleeve. 'That upset me, to be honest with you,' he told Daniels. 'Having played all of those songs and practised them and refined them, as songs do evolve over a long period of time, it was a real bit of a pisser.'

Talking of the sleeve, such 'an elaborate and pseudo-gothic' (as Raven's John Gallagher puts it) album required more than a glorified bottle top to bring it visually to life, and Patrick Woodroffe's iconic image of one of the fallen angels, trapped in Hell and wracked in pain, was to be the first of many impressive and/or eye-catching Judas Priest sleeves. Look closely at the figure (which one wag once unkindly suggested looked like he was having a stretch after an afternoon nap) and around his neck is the pendant – The Devil's Pitchfork – which would later become one of the band's most recognisable emblems, appearing for example on the rear sleeve of 1984's *Defenders Of The Faith* and even forming the base of Halford's replacement Tim 'Ripper' Owens' mike stand.

Before looking at the album, it's worth noting that there's some debate as to how to play it. Although Sides A and B are clearly marked on the record itself, with Side A opening with 'Victim Of Changes' and Side B starting with 'Prelude', the original sleeve itself appears to indicate the opposite – that 'Prelude' through to 'Island Of Domination' should be the first side. Songs are listed in what has become to be the accepted running order, though to be honest playing the album as listed on the sleeve ('Prelude' / 'Tyrant' / 'Genocide' / 'Epitaph' / 'Island Of Domination' / 'Victim Of Changes' / 'Ripper' / 'Dreamer Deceiver'/'Deceiver') makes for a much more satisfying and 'complete' experience. Try it and see.

'Victim Of Changes' (Downing / Halford / Tipton / Atkins)

It comes as no surprise that the opener 'Victim Of Changes' – credited to Downing /Halford /Tipton / Atkins – is actually two songs glued together.

'Whiskey Woman' was an old Atkins composition, road-tested to perfection during the early days, and 'Red Light Lady' was a slower Rob Halford composition from Hiroshima days. Interesting on their own, put together they've become one of the most enduring and instantly recognisable heavy metal songs of all time.

''Victim Of Changes' is just an epic, full-stop,' notes Satan's Russ Tippins:

> *It's the sort of thing that you'd normally save for the end of the album, and it must have been quite a brave move opening the record with such a long track. 'Victim Of Changes' is my favourite song – not that that's ever an easy question to ask of any Judas Priest fan! But even now, when it comes on it never fails to set the hairs on end, and send the shivers down the back, especially that middle section where it goes right down. That's just heavenly.*

'**Ripper** (Tipton)'

The shorter, leaner 'Ripper' cools things off, despite the opening eight notes screeching in like a banshee and overpowering the climax to 'Victim Of Changes'. Like 'Breaking The Law' several years later Glenn Tipton's first solo contribution to the catalogue is, in reality, a triumph of style over substance as it chugs along blissfully with nothing really happening for less than three minutes and yet it still leaves its mark on the listener.

One thing Downing learned from his experiences during the recording of *Rocka Rolla* was that he felt pressure in the studio environment that wasn't there when he played live. As an experiment, he practised the middle section of the song pretending he was playing live, head flung back, throwing the shapes and really giving it some, and it was at this point that the young Chris Tsangarides walked in on him wondering what was going on.

Despite its enduring place both in the hearts of Priest fans and in the band's live set, 'Ripper', one of Priest's most famous songs, has been the target of more than its fair share of criticism over the years. Although its historical content and rather vaudeville lyrics bring to mind more an over-played Victorian melodrama than a contemporary horror, 'Ripper' is still touted from time to time as an example of the misogyny that supposedly lurks at the heart of metal.

Sad Wings Of Destiny didn't really offer the record label much choice in terms of a single so 'Ripper' was trotted out as the album's token 7", backed by 'Island Of Domination'; unsurprisingly, it failed to make any headway chartwise.

'Dreamer Deceiver' / **'Deceiver'** (Downing / Halford / Tipton)

The vinyl album's first side is brought to a more than satisfactory conclusion with the eight-and-three-quarter minute coupling of 'Dreamer Deceiver' and 'Deceiver' which, let's be fair, are really just one song (although presented this way the songwriters get two bites at the publishing cherry). A truly great offering in the band's early catalogue, it's a real shame that this pairing didn't last very long in the band's live set as taken as a whole they represent the very essence of Judas Priest. The opening is slow and determined with beautifully fluid soloing and superb whisper-to-scream vocals which build things up for an explosion of pure energy as Halford's scream ushers in 'Deceiver', which shakes its fist aggressively for a couple of minutes and then retires abruptly, giving way to a short, acoustic coda.

Lyrically, there's a bit of a clunker when Halford relates that in the cosmos 'there is a single sonic sound' but don't let that spoil one of the band's early milestones. Both parts of the saga are credited to Downing /Halford / Tipton on later pressings of the record and CD, although Atkins clarifies in his autobiography that 'Dreamer Deceiver' was one of his riffs.

'The thing about 'Dreamer Deceiver' and 'Deceiver' is that they're both good songs in their own right,' says Russ Tippins, 'but the way they are linked made them so much better. The whole is much much more than just the sum of its parts.'

'Prelude' (Tipton)

So, if you go with the running order as suggested on the LP itself, Side Two opens with this two-minute piano-based composition adorned with a fluid guitar lead run atop it. The tape is slowed for dramatic effect and gives way to…

'Tyrant' (Tipton / Halford)

One of the band's most enduring songs and a highlight – well, one of the many – of the 1979 *Unleashed In The East* live album. The titular tyrant is a warlord hell-bent on world domination, and while the lyrics don't stand up to too much scrutiny, there's plenty to keep the two guitarists busy, and the twin guitar lead that follows the third chorus is a work of sublime beauty. Things don't get much better than this.

'Genocide' (Tipton / Halford / Downing)

Another battle song, this time told from the perspective of the victims or the oppressed. Much more malevolent than anything else on the album, and lyrically much darker (with the line 'Sin After Sin I have endured' giving the band the title of their next album). If 'Tyrant' showcased Downing and Tipton, then 'Genocide' was more about Halford's range. The time-change at the four-minute mark makes for an interesting coda, although that then is trumped by the almost bluesy ending to the song.

Onstage, 'Genocide' often featured Halford firing a machine gun, a prop that was eventually phased out as more and more venue owners worried that the ejected shell casings might injure members of the audience.

'Epitaph' (Tipton)

'Epitaph', again a Tipton solo composition, is the album's weakest link, although later ballads like 'Last Rose Of Summer' and 'Before The Dawn' can trace their DNA back to this piano-based offering. The song's character reflects on his life, alone in his solitude as people pass him by without even noticing him, and the song's moral is that we all become that person in the end. It's on this song that the Queen-isms shine through most brightly, not being that dissimilar to Freddie Mercury's 'Lily Of The Valley'. In fact, you could make a convincing argument for showing how this and the following track 'Island Of Domination' mirror almost perfectly the effect Messrs Mercury, May, Deacon and Taylor achieved with the soft-but-soaring 'Lily Of The Valley' and the full-frontal aggression of 'Now I'm Here' on their November 1974 *Sheer Heart Attack* album, which must have been on Priest's radar.

'Island Of Domination' (Downing / Halford / Tipton)

A belligerent but enjoyable way to round things off, a metal slap in the face after the more, well, pretentious preceding cut to which it's conjoined, 'Island Of Domination' (like 'Dreamer Deceiver' / 'Deceiver') dropped out of the live set way too early. Taken out of context, some critics now like to present 'Island Of Domination' as an early indication of Halford's sexual fetishism, probably arising from the line 'lashings of strappings with beatings competing to win'. I suppose, the onstage introduction at Reading of 'for those out there who like to be dominated…' wouldn't detract from this view, although the song is more about an Inquisition-style torment and from the 'Skyrider supersonic flyer / Night driver demon of desire' couplet not for the last time a science fiction angle arises. The complete change of tempo at the 2:20 mark is a real curve-ball until the band veer back into the main riff and crash 'n' burn to the end. The album closes with Halford's reverb fade.

Post Album Events

Diamond Head's Brian Tatler first saw the band in 1975, before *Sad Wings Of Destiny* had been recorded:

> *I don't remember much about that gig, being such a long time ago, but what I do remember was that it was at Birmingham Town Hall [which dates it to 12 April] and that it was Judas Priest supporting Budgie; and I'm pretty sure it was about 70p to get in. I mean, what a bargain! I do remember that Rob Halford had flowing, straight long blonde hair – because of course, it was very short later, and that's kind of how you see him when you think of him – and I remember K.K. Downing played a Stratocaster with a whammy bar, because he does those mad solos with the feedback and stuff; and I'm sure he had a white fedora on, a white hat, so he'd stand out. I can't remember the other guys! But I do remember the hat – the cat in the hat! I liked them there and then. I'd come to see Budgie, but because Priest are a Birmingham band I might have heard of them, but once I saw them I thought they were great. And then, of course, Sad Wings Of Destiny came out, and I bought that. Thinking about it, I think I might have bought the single first, as they'd released 'Ripper' with*

'Island Of Domination' on the B-side. So once I heard that I thought, that's fantastic, I've got to buy that album.

I think that's their best, though. It's a brilliant album, especially for the time. And 'Island Of Domination' was always my favourite track, I think because of the riff, that little riff, in the verse. I used to play it to death. And there's that slow passage in the middle, that was such a mean riff, I thought that was great. We used to try to cover 'Ripper' in my bedroom in the early days of Diamond Head. We tried to do that one mainly because of that chug-chug-chugging riff. But it would get to a point where I couldn't play it anymore, because that guitar piece which is kind of like the solo in the middle, I found I couldn't figure all that out, and the song would just collapse! But we all liked that track a lot. And of course 'Victim Of Changes' is a marvellous song. I think there's a bit of Diamond Head there – we poached a bit of 'Victim Of Changes' for a Diamond Head song. I think the way it goes to the bridge, where it goes from A to E, I think we had that for 'Sucking My Love'.

When asked about the seeming leap in songwriting between the first two albums K.K. Downing is quite hesitant, and even questions the assertion. 'Was there a leap? I don't know … I know we were playing 'Victim Of Changes' when Al Atkins was in the band. So some of the important stuff on *Sad Wings Of Destiny* didn't even make it onto the first album, although it was being played live at the same time.' The point is that although the records do sound different, a lot of the material co-existed. 'I don't even know which is my favourite now,' he says of the two Gull releases. 'I'd have to go back to the albums and listen to them again because you don't really, do you?'

Although some sources claim that *Sad Wings Of Destiny* broke into the UK Top 50, this is incorrect, and the album charts compilers never lost any sleep over it at all, although as far as Gull were concerned the relationship was ticking along quite nicely. In *Defenders Of The Faith*, David Howells told Neil Daniels: 'We signed, developed and helped them to become the Judas Priest the world has known for thirty years. It's very easy to lose an act like that … All the signs were there after *Sad Wings Of Destiny* came out. All the groundwork had been done. But the band were, literally, starving. Downing recalls that they asked Gull for a wage, £25 per week, and were turned down. 'We were struggling to pay for petrol to get to the next gig. We couldn't stay with Gull, but we refused to give in. Gull advanced us £2,000 per album – but we went to CBS and got £60,000 almost overnight.'

The Best Of Judas Priest – The Gull Years Revisited

In *Sounds,* in September 1984 a reader by name of Garry Sharpe (I'm guessing this was the author / journalist who died in 2010) wrote a piece on Judas Priest rarities, including US singles and the 1975 Reading highlight 'Mother Sun'. 'Most Priest freaks know that it exists in studio form, and last month I was privileged actually to hear it, courtesy of Gull's David Howell. Although it has often been suggested that they should release the track in 12" form, the label have not done so – mainly in fairness to the band, as the cut is just a studio demo featuring Rob's vocal and one guitar – that's all.'

Gull Records weren't, however, afraid to cash in on their former act's new-found fame (although at this stage the phrase 'you ain't seen nothing yet' springs to mind) by releasing *The Best Of Judas Priest* in February 1978. This was a single album which brought together 'Dying To Meet You', 'Never Satisfied' and 'Rocka Rolla' from the first album with 'Victim Of Changes', 'Island Of Domination', 'Ripper' and 'Deceiver' from *Sad Wings Of Destiny* making up Side Two. A rather tasty picture disc version of the album was also made available later (apparently just a limited pressing of 5,000 copies), but the big bonus was that the final track on Side One was the band's unreleased first stab at 'Diamonds And Rust'. This was added as the bait to make the record more attractive to the fans who already possessed the original Gull LPs.

Exactly when this was first recorded by Judas Priest is open to debate. Neil Daniels' *Defenders Of The Faith* presents two sides to the story. On the one hand, *Sad Wings Of Destiny* co-producer Geraint Hughes stated that it pre-dated the band's second album. 'We recorded a single at Morgan Studios earlier that year,' he said, in relation to his work on Sad Wings…, 'a cover of the Joan Baez song 'Diamonds And Rust'.' Label manager David Howells had a different slant on things, telling Daniels, ''Diamonds And Rust' was I believe the only time I suggested Judas Priest record someone else's song. After all, they weren't short of good songs themselves. It was just that I thought Joan Baez's 'Diamonds And Rust' would complement their own material and make a good single. Incidentally, my memory tells me that it was the last track recorded by the band for Gull, rather than coming before *Sad Wings Of Destiny*.'

As time has dulled memories, Chris Tsangarides can't recall the exact sequence either. 'That was recorded, I think,' he said, hesitantly, 'after we finished the record and then we came back in to do it [which ties in with Howell's recollection]. I was the assistant again on that. Or was it before we finished the album? I can't remember now. It wasn't released on the album, but it was definitely around that time because I remember being there, doing it. But the engineer on that was Martin Levan who is a great chap and who taught me a whole load of things. He was really my mentor.'

The 1987 CD version added 'Epitaph' and 'One For The Road', while the 2001 CD was expanded further by the addition of eight interview tracks featuring original drummer John Hinch, which was a step too far. The band's displeasure is best summarised in the following disclaimer which was posted on the official Judas Priest website:

> *Gull Records through many subsidiary companies are releasing sub-standard re-hashes of these first two albums under different guises. If for instance, anyone out there has bought their* Judas Priest – The Best Of – Insight Series, *then they would find that 50% of the album consists of a mindless interview with John Hinch, an ex-drummer with Priest who we had to let go because he was musically inadequate. The interview is not only misleading but full of rubbish and false information. They, however, have cleverly tracklisted the back cover, so it appears that other band members are involved and as though it contains new material. It's just one example of how Gull Records are greedily continually exploiting and misleading the fans out there, and unfortunately, we cannot control it or stop them – but we can strongly advise you not to waste your money buying tracks you will already have under the original album titles. They have nothing new to offer and are just trying to cash in on the Priest name – so check out any CD with their name on it before buying.*

Back in the twentieth century, as the band's star continued to rise, a 12 inch single combining 'Victim Of Changes', 'Ripper' and 'Never Satisfied' was issued in August 1980, with a further 12" single featuring 'Tyrant', 'Rocka Rolla' and 'Genocide' following in June 1983. Both came in picture sleeves although 'Tyrant' was pressed in highly collectable white vinyl, and the release of the first single in particular probably left many new converts to the cause reading the songwriting credits and wondering who on earth 'Atkins' might be. The 1981 release *Hero Hero* (with its terrifically stirring fantasy cover of a warrior striding forth into battle, again by Melvyn Gant of *The Steel Tsar* fame) appeared as a double LP featuring most, but not all, of those first two albums (with the by now obligatory version of 'Diamonds And Rust' making the cut). 1989's *The Collection* (which used the same cover remixed) and 2000's *Genocide* (a rather childishly envisioned graveyard and skull) both double-packed *Rocka Rolla* and *Sad Wings Of Destiny*, ensuring that neither album was out of print for very long while endlessly mining the back catalogue for all it was worth.

Meanwhile, the band themselves did nothing to reclaim the early material. If anything from the Gull years appeared on an 'official' Priest compilation, it was only a live version of a track or two from *Sad Wings Of Destiny*. Despite being continually overlooked by CBS records for many years in the many compilations and collections of the band's material, the heritage of the two Gull releases was finally recognised when they were belatedly included in the Complete Albums Collection box set in 2012. This was a seventeen-CD box set which tied in with the Epitaph tour on which the band played at least one song from every album fronted by Rob Halford.

Sin After Sin (1977)

Personnel:
Glenn Tipton: guitars
Robert Halford: vocals
K.K. Downing: guitars
Ian Hill: bass guitar
Special thanks to Simon Phillips: drums/percussion
Record label: CBS
Recorded at Ramport Studios, Battersea, London, January 1977
Produced by: Roger Glover/Judas Priest
Release date: 23 April 1977
Highest chart positions: UK: 23, US: did not chart
Running time: 40:07

> ***An album that could stop an advancing Chieftain tank in its tracks and shake it apart into a pile of nuts 'n' bolts...*** Geoff Barton, *Sounds'* album review

Gull Records' David Howells was correct when he said that all the groundwork had been done for the band, but if Judas Priest were to morph into Metal Gods truly they would need a much firmer foundation than anything Gull could offer. And the proof of the pudding was seeing *Sin After Sin* enter the UK charts on 14 May 1977 for a six-week run.

Rob Halford, K.K. Downing, Glenn Tipton and Ian Hill took two things to CBS Records. The first was the idea for a title – Sin After Sin being the opening line of the spoken word passage in 'Genocide' – and the second was the notion of recording Joan Baez's 'Diamonds And Rust'. As mentioned previously, this had already been committed to tape by the band for Gull Records and was later issued by the label on their *The Best Of Judas Priest* album in 1978. The one thing the band didn't take to CBS was drummer Alan Moore. Well, that's not 100% true, but before their first album for the label had been completed Moore had left for a second time and a 'situation vacant' sign was hanging above the drum kit once more.

Despite a bigger label and a bigger budget, *Sin After Sin* didn't come easy at first. In 2007 Tipton admitted to Dave Ling in Classic Rock Presents Heavy Metal that 'although *Sin After Sin* was a good album that featured 'Dissident Aggressor' and 'Starbreaker', it wasn't abounding with songs.' Although when he continued, 'and because Roger Glover came in halfway through it sounded a bit thin,' he was perhaps being – at least in relation to the producer's role – a little economical with the truth, because if there are any shortcomings on *Sin After Sin* the band really have to shoulder a lot of the responsibility.

Roger Glover was an ideal candidate for the producer's chair. Having been forced to leave Deep Purple to make way for new blood after the band's 1973 Japanese tour, Glover already had well over a dozen production credits to his name by the time he was approached to work with Judas Priest on their third album. Downing admits in his autobiography that it was the label's idea to engage Glover, and that having him on board might give them some kudos in what he called a 'Deep-Purple-guy-produces-Judas-Priest way. We were fine with that ... even though none of us had a comprehensive idea what Roger's credentials as a producer were.' The guitarist continues that Glover was 'a lovely guy and great to work with,' although that glosses over Glover's account in Martin Popoff's *Heavy Metal Painkillers*, which indicated that the producer realised that he wasn't actually wanted as, after two albums which didn't really capture their sound, the musicians were adamant that they would handle the task themselves. Such was the band's insistence that at the end of the first meeting producer and band parted company amicably.

'And that's all there was until a month or two later when they were actually in the studio, and I got a call begging for help basically,' recalled Glover to Popoff. 'They'd been in the studio for like two weeks, and in the process, they'd sacked the drummer, and they had six studio days left. So I got in the car and went down to the studio and said, "well, play me what you've got". And they played me what they had, and it was awful. There was nothing really worth salvaging. And I said, "right, what do you want to do?" And they said, "well, we have six days and we're going to get Simon Phillips," who I happen to know anyway, and I said, "right, well we're going to start from scratch, and we're going to do it really quick," and boom, we did. So we recorded everything again.'

The album was recorded at Ramport Studios in Battersea, London (a facility owned by The Who and home to an aquarium full of poisonous fish, apparently), in January 1977 and released the following April. Some pre-production took place first at Pinewood Studios, more famous for making movies than making music, and the vacancy was filled by Simon Phillips. Phillips is the drummer's drummer, a man who can seemingly play anything at the drop of a hat and whose name has gone on to appear on countless albums over the years (including hooking up again with Roger Glover on Michael Schenker's first solo LP in 1980) as a musician and also latterly as a producer. There weren't even any demos to guide the drummer. 'Glenn just had all the songs in his head, and we went through them,' he told Popoff. 'I would play along, and when there was a riff to learn, we would stop, he'd show me the riff a couple of times, and we would carry on.'

The cover – which is much, much better suited to an LP than to a CD where it loses its visual impact – was created by Bob Carlos Clarke, an Irish-born photographer by that time living in London who would go on to become one of the leading photographers of his age. Hi is often described as 'Britain's Answer To Helmut Newton,' even though he wasn't actually British and he died in 2006. In his book *Shooting Sex* (the field in which he was to make his name) he reminisces:

> *At this point, my most vital source of visual inspiration was album sleeves. I can't recall much of the music, but the covers are with me for*

> *eternity:* Trout Mask Replica, Houses Of The Holy, King Crimson, Sticky Fingers ... *I had no idea that in a few years I'd be struggling to shoot acts that included Judas Priest, Ozzy Osbourne, Meat Loaf, and The Who...*

The result is more rococo than rock, and as Martin Popoff points out in *Fade To Black* the only real nod to metaldom is the skull that adorns the sepulchre doorway (and which appears on the shore on the rear cover distance image). Art direction is credited to Roslaw Szaybo, the chief artistic director at CBS, who would continue to work with Priest on their next few albums, producing ever more striking images.

The grace and glory of *Sin After Sin* weren't missed by either public or press, and writing for *Sounds* Geoff Barton, who would go on to be one of the band's most vocal supporters, reviewed the album in April 1977 and gave it the full five-star accolade:

> *Judas Priest have come of age. Away from the stumbling block of Decca's so-called progressive label, Gull records; away from their disastrous, Roger [sic] Bain produced debut album release* Rocka Rolla*; away from even much-better-but-sadly-it-didn't-receive-the-attention-it-deserved second LP* Sad Wings Of Destiny. *Away from all the uncertain moments of the past and into the safe arms of CBS records and Roger Glover. The result? A third cataclysmic platter* Sin After Sin, *an album that could stop an advancing Chieftain tank in its tracks and shake it apart into a pile of nuts 'n' bolts. Brummie metal merchants Judas Priest have, with this LP, usurped Black Sabbath's throne with the minimum of bloodshed but with a maximum of volume. While the Sabs – sadly – now flounder in riff-churning, peace sign flashing monotony, Judas Priest fight to lace doom-laden, menacing heavy rock music with some fresh instrumental angles, some variation and, above all else, some excitement...*

After a track-by-track rundown, Barton concluded:

> *And while singer Rob Halford goes over the top with the vocal gymnastics at times, and while Roger Glover's largely commendable production plays little attention to the subtleties of Judas Priest's music (for subtleties there are),* Sin After Sin *remains the most powerful British heavy rock release for years.*

There's no doubting that a review such as this would have piqued the interest of even the least-enquiring rock fan of the mid-Seventies. The reviewer's point was well made, and CBS's faith in the band was vindicated (as come to that, was the band's faith in themselves). On 14 May 1977, Judas Priest broke into the album charts for the first time. *Sin After Sin* would go on to peak at Number 23, spending six weeks basking in national glory, and the band finally had an album which was making people sit up and listen. If *Rocka Rolla* was the stroll across through the funfair and *Sad Wings Of Destiny* was the ticket booth, *Sin After Sin* was the start of the roller-coaster ride that would take five guys from Birmingham (well, four Brummies and assorted drummers) around the world. Several times.

'Sinner' (Tipton / Halford)

As with *Sad Wings Of Destiny* before it, *Sin After Sin* opens with the album's longest and least commercial cut – try getting a single edit out of this bellicose bad boy! As if making a statement of intent the new Priest album was to open with an exhilarating six-and-a-half minutes of pure metal adrenaline with no let-ups, no quarter, and the song would go on to be a live staple for some years, really coming into its own onstage and being another of the highlights on *Unleashed In The East*.

Although it's six-and-three-quarter minutes long, 'Sinner' is quite short when you consider just how much is packed into it. A couple of riff-driven verses, a bridge and then a powerful solo section which allows Downing to run rampage (possibly with images of Jimi Hendrix in his head), accompanied towards the end by his singer, almost drowned in reverb. The band gear back up into the song once more and with just one more guitar break race to the song's frenetic conclusion. Perfection.

'Diamonds And Rust' (Joan Baez)

Confusion reigns! Downing claims in his book that he was told that Roger Glover suggested covering 'Diamonds And Rust', although reckoned that 'this was the label's idea and that they were just using the man on the ground, Roger, as their spokesperson.' He goes on to indicate that he wasn't that enthusiastic at first ('no, we should leave it alone'), although all this seems at odds with the fact that they'd already taped it once before.

However, what's not in doubt is that, although the band followed the song's general ethos, they made it their own, streamlining it, upping the tempo, cutting verses and adding a storming climax, and were so successful that many fans believed it was self-penned. It's actually from the album of the same name, recorded in January 1975 and released the following April, with Joan Baez writing about another Robert – Robert Zimmerman. Whether Halford had Bob Dylan in mind when he almost spits out some of the lines is probably unlikely.

It's positioning on the album is rather odd, sandwiched between two more frenetic outings, and you get the feeling that it had to go somewhere so this was as good a place as anywhere else and does give the original vinyl's first side a hard-soft-hard-soft balance. In the later Ripper Owens' years, the band stripped the song back to its acoustic roots, slowing it down and offering more of a faithful rendition, albeit still with their own arrangement. A nice idea, but it lacked the authority with which the earlier line-up had imbued the song.

'Starbreaker' (Tipton / Halford / Downing)

Given its drum intro, it's perhaps little surprise that 'Starbreaker' would go on to highlight the drummer onstage and incorporate a brief solo from the band's next skinbeater, Les Binks. On record though 'Starbreaker' is a bit of a lightweight, and certainly not as heavy as it would turn out to be when it entered the live set. Vocally, it's a bit of a monster though, with Halford soaring over the melody, and it features an early example of the dynamic twin leads from the guitar duo that Downing so craved, as well as Deep Purple-esque 'Black Night' style handclaps, presumably brought to the mix by Glover. Indeed, it's interesting/infuriating that as the singer hits those really high spine-tingling notes that make live versions so appealing – until they give way to the drum solo, that is – in the studio Glover was already working the faders, thus robbing the track of some of its glory.

'Last Rose Of Summer' (Halford / Tipton)

Sin After Sin was the album on which the band – Halford in particular – finally got their Queen pretensions out of their systems with two offerings, the first of which occurred as Side One's closing cut. It's a nice song, a twee song, and maybe after the previous work-out it was thought that listeners might need a breather, but it's about as far removed from 'Sinner' as it's possible to be. Dubbed 'dispensably dorkish and overly romantic' by *Sounds*' reviewer Geoff Barton, the song does again allow Halford to demonstrate his astonishing range, but at over five minutes long it does outstay its welcome, and in his autobiography Downing describes the song as a weakness, thinking 'this sucks. We sound too much like Queen.' There is no record of the song ever being played live, which is probably for the best, really.

'Let Us Prey' / 'Call For The Priest' (Halford / Downing / Tipton)

In fact, 'Last Rose Of Summer' is actually a sucker-punch, because when (in days gone by) you'd flipped the record over *Sin After Sin* turns rather nasty. The brief Queen-tinged intro 'Let Us Prey' gives way to the malevolence of 'Call For The Priest', a self-referential one-time set opener and the first real example of Halford whipping up a storm with this tongue-twisting avalanche of syllables:

> *When your back's to the wall come along one and all, we shall fight all the slander that's penned*
> *It's us we shall choose, let the bigoted lose, for our triumph's the means to their end*

The band thunder in at a gallop, with Phillips thrashing his kit to within an inch of its life, and with duelling guitars, a twin lead, and speed a-plenty this is the perfect piece to play to anyone who thinks playing fast wasn't invented until the Eighties.

It's worth noting that there was a mistake on the original pressing, in that the sleeve listed 'Let Us Prey' as the first cut on Side Two, followed by 'Call For The Priest/Raw Deal'. 'Let Us Prey' is merely a brief instrumental intro, but as the LP didn't come with a lyric sheet, you wouldn't know. This accounts for what appears to be an error in Geoff Barton's 1977 review where he refers to 'Let Us Prey' as 'maniacally speedy guitar riff, high pitched vocals, appropriate gasp-to-catch-a-breath pauses, great song construction-destruction,' and then describes 'Call For The Priest'/'Raw Deal' as 'weighty, leaden, cumbersome, metallic overload').

'Raw Deal' (Halford / Tipton)

'Raw Deal' is a slower and scuzzier song, as dirty as the floor of the bar in which its action takes place. As the song namechecks New York's Fire Island, an area known for its gay scene it's another piece that's often used as early evidence of Halford expressing his sexuality through his lyrics. Although at the time of recording *Sin After Sin* the band hadn't actually been across the Atlantic, there were sufficient popular cultural references to Fire Island for Halford to be aware of it. And for those who love tangled knots and conspiracy theories, in 1969 there was a film *Last Summer* set on Fire Island which tackled awakening sexuality in adolescents, although was heterosexual in nature. But *Last Summer*? 'Last Rose Of Summer'? Fire Island? Is there a link there somewhere? The trouble is that you can spend all day interpreting lyrics that are well written and obtuse and still end up no further forward.

Whatever the lyrical content, 'Raw Deal' is still a hefty chunk of metal, especially when it drops the tempo and the vocals are double-tracked and layered. Given the treasures on offer on this side of the record it's often overlooked, but 'Raw Deal' is a track deserving of credit.

'Here Come The Tears' (Halford / Tipton)

'Here Come The Tears' seems at first to be another chip off the Queen-adoring 'Epitaph' block, but give it a minute or so, and an acoustic riff with piano accompaniment makes for a plaintive Priest song. Once it steps up and takes on its repetitive refrain, introduced by and interwoven with a classic Priest guitar solo it betrays more than just a hint of malevolence as the character who just wants 'to be loved' slips away into eternal peace. The high-pitched vocals give way to an explosion and then...

'Dissident Aggressor' (Tipton / Halford / Downing)

...Rising from the ashes comes 'Dissident Aggressor'. As *Sin After Sin* mimicked its predecessor in its opening, it follows the same path at the end with the ballad this time giving way to a final slice of ferociousness. A song of actually very few words, 'Dissident Aggressor' takes a sci-fi concept and interweaves the then divided city of Berlin with the band behind Halford creating a solid wall of fire over the belligerent vocal delivery. Downing and Tipton trade solos, while behind them Hill and Phillips just about keep the wheels from falling off.

'Dissident Aggressor' went on to be nobly covered by Slayer on their 1988 *South Of Heaven* album, and in 2010 won Judas Priest a Grammy for 'Best Metal Performance' for their rendition of the song on the otherwise rather disappointing 2009 *A Touch Of Evil – Live* album.

Post Album Events

With a new label and a chart-pleasing album, world domination beckoned. But first off Messrs. Halford, Downing, Tipton and Hill needed to fill the vacancy behind the drum stool. Although they were more than keen enough to recruit Simon Phillips, the drummer was already committed to working with Jack Bruce. According to Neil Daniels' *Defenders Of The Faith* it was at Glover's suggestion that the band hired drummer Les Binks, as Glover 'knew Les Binks very well, having worked with him on several projects. These include *The Butterfly Ball And The Grasshopper's Feast*' and also on the *Wizards' Convention* gathering which featured Glover alongside other ex-Deep Purple members as well as Binks and his Fancy bandmates Mo Foster and Ray Fenwick. Both these musicians weave in and out of the Seventies' Deep Purple splinter bands (and for complete trivia, Foster would play bass on Michael Schenker's first album after leaving UFO, alongside Simon Phillips, with Glover in the producer's chair). Downing recalled it differently to Steve Gett, telling the author that 'we held a series for auditions in London and eventually found Les Binks,' or James Leslie Binks as he was known to his mum, a drummer who ironically shares the same date of birth – 5 April 1948 – as the guy who would succeed him. In his autobiography, Downing draws a pencil portrait of a man, again from the session scene, 'rooted in jazz [who] could play absolutely anything. He was a good guy too: Irish, reserved, a vegetarian…'

The *Sin After Sin* tour kicked off with the release of the record in April and saw the band's first US dates. After a month or so in the UK, supported by fellow Brummies Magnum whose first album *Kingdom Of Madness* had been recorded, but in true Jet records fashion wouldn't see the light of day until August 1978. The band then hopped across the Atlantic and spent the summer in the States, the tour commencing on 17 June in Amarillo, Texas, and running through to the end of July with the band providing support on some very mismatched bills to the likes of REO Speedwagon, Foreigner and Ted Nugent. Having based their expectations of America on TV programmes the musicians found the tour a massive culture shock. However, playing to 7,000 to 8,000 seat auditoria where (to be generous) in the UK the biggest venues probably held no more than 2,000 people more than made up for Downing's complaint to Steve Gett that he 'couldn't stand the food at all and really missed being able to get regular things like sausage and tomato sandwiches.' Ah, the Brits abroad… This is the man who, Chris Tsangarides once told Paul Britton, recorded *Sad Wings Of Destiny* on a diet of 'double cheese on toast and mashed spuds.'

Although there are no official live recordings from this era, there's a bootleg of the show from the Freeman Coliseum in San Antonio, Texas, on 21 June with a very tasty set consisting of 'Let Us Prey/Call For The Priest' / 'Victim Of Changes' / 'Diamonds And Rust' / 'The Ripper' / 'Sinner' / 'Genocide' / 'Starbreaker'. The icing on the tour cake was yet to come, though, as two more dates were added to the end of the schedule, on 23 and 24 July, supporting

Led Zeppelin in San Francisco at the *Day On The Green Festival*. Despite the fact that Priest came on unfeasibly early – before midday – the festival put them in front of around 60,000 people each day which can't have done their burgeoning profile on the West Coast any harm at all.

The album's single 'Diamonds And Rust' b/w 'Dissident Aggressor', released the same month as *Sin After Sin* in April 1977, failed to match the achievements of its parent album. Despite the high hopes CBS must have had for this sure-fire success (and don't forget, Gull Records had also thought this would be a hit) 'Diamonds And Rust' failed to tickle even the lowest regions of the singles charts and was soon banished to obscurity.

But there's no rest for the wicked, and as the band members' 1977 diaries already had 'record new album' scribbled through October's and November's pages, they had plenty of work to do before they could take a break and start writing their Christmas present lists.

Stained Class (1978)

Personnel:
Robert Halford: vocals
Glen [sic] Tipton: guitars, vocals
K.K. Downing: guitars
Ian Hill: bass guitar
Les Binks: drums
Record label: CBS
Recorded at Chipping Norton Studios, Oxfordshire, Advision Studios, Trident Studios, and Utopia Studios, London, October/November 1977
Produced by: Dennis MacKay and Judas Priest except 'Better By You Better Than Me' by James Guthrie and Judas Priest
Release date: 10 February 1978
Highest chart positions: UK: 27, US: 173
Running time: 43:40

> *I loved* Sad Wings Of Destiny *for the amazing bottom end it generated out of my stereo, but my all-time favourite album of theirs is* Stained Class *for the amazing songs that are on that record. I still don't think those records have ever been bettered by any metal band* – Lips, Anvil

Judas Priest's fourth album *Stained Class* marked the end of the first phase of the band's career. It was after this that Rob Halford, Glenn Tipton, K.K. Downing, Ian Hill and Les Binks – whose contribution to the album was deemed to be immense, both as drummer and co-writer of one of the band's most enduring songs – moved away from the more progressive material that been so overt on *Sin After Sin* and even more overt on *Sad Wings Of Destiny,* and began to write songs which said what they had to say in four minutes or less.

Released in February 1978, and sitting comfortably between the major label breakthrough *Sin After Sin* and the image-conscious *Killing Machine*, *Stained Class* is the Priest album which often tends to get overlooked. 'I think we were still looking for the right sound, which we hadn't quite got together,' Rob Halford told Steve Gett in 1984. 'We were in the midst of trying to get away from the lengthy, post-early-Seventies, nine-minute epic songs and we didn't quite know where to go. Looking back,' he said, quite tellingly, 'I'd say we were searching for our real identities.'

The album was recorded with producer Dennis MacKay largely at Chipping Norton Studios in Oxfordshire, in October and November 1977. MacKay was an experienced engineer who'd then moved on to produce an eclectic range of artists including Tommy Bolin (producing both *Teaser* and *Private Eyes*), Gong (*Expresso* and *Gazeuse!*) and Brand X (*Moroccan Roll*) prior to getting the job with Priest. It was also the first album to feature Les Binks, who would occupy the drum stool for the foreseeable future, setting a record for percussive longevity in the band. Writing in *Classic Rock*, Al King revealed that MacKay was meticulous in his approach, and started with just the new boy. 'The foundation is the most important,' said the producer, recalling that 'Les Binks was the first to arrive at Chipping Norton and was understandably a little bit nervous... It took two whole days to get the drum sounds right, and throughout the recording, Les re-tuned his drums every twenty minutes to maintain it.' On the third day, the guitarists arrived, and MacKay played back what they'd achieved. 'They listened stony faced and expressionless. I was rather worried.' However, it appears that Tipton and Downing were so impressed with what they heard that a decision was made to kick off *Stained Class* with 'Exciter''s opening fusillade of drums.

Six more days of sorting the guitar speaker cabinets and positioning microphones followed before everyone was ready to rock 'n' roll. And rock 'n' roll they did. Self-confessed *Sad Wings Of Destiny* addict and ex-Year Of the Goat guitarist Per Broddesson is also a big fan of *Stained Class*. 'There comes a time when the only thing that'll satisfy your need to hear some Judas Priest is to dig out your old beat-up copy of *Stained Class* on vinyl. And let me tell you straight away if your copy is not beaten up and scruffy you have either not given it the full treatment it deserves, or you're more of a nerd with your collection than you need to be,' he laughs, before jabbing the air with his index finger. 'Understand this: if *Sad Wings Of Destiny* is so good that you've worn out at least five copies, *Stained Class* is so good that you always need to have a pristine back-up copy readily available. This album needs to be played often, and played loud. There are a number of similarities between these two albums, but probably the biggest is the fact that you can't really single out any specific tracks as being better than any other. They are all just perfect as they are. The main difference though lies in the fact that where *Sad Wings Of Destiny* is more in the vein of progressive Seventies rock, *Stained Class* lies firmly rooted in early heavy metal, with the emphasis on both the heavy and the metal.'

There are no passengers on the *Stained Class* train. It's pretty much the aural equivalent of being locked in your favourite sweet shop with guaranteed, indefinite protection against tooth decay. There's nothing superfluous on the album – everything brings something to the table. Aside from the music, the album is famous for two things in particular. The first is that the band's new logo made its appearance for the first time, occupying the top right-hand corner of Roslaw Szaybo striking design and banishing the gothic script of the previous two albums and remaining in place on the front of every official release that featured Halford until 2008's Nostrdamus. It's also the album on which Ian Hill switched to playing with a plectrum, although this doesn't make it particularly noteworthy. 'It didn't matter how hard I hit the strings with my fingers, it got mixed in with the guitars,' he told Al King. 'If you hit it with a pick you get that defined attack.' For all that though, it was the last time he'd receive a writing credit on a Judas Priest album.

'Exciter' (Tipton / Halford)

One of the most exciting and frenetic songs ever put to vinyl, 'Exciter' showcases Judas Priest at their best. The opening drum onslaught is the perfect introduction to new boy Les Binks, the fast 'n' furious pace of the song illustrates just what the band can do when they are let off the leash, and then there's Halford at his best, screeching the final lines at a pitch only metal fans and dogs can hear. Apparently, 90 per cent of the vocal performances were done in one take.

Even now, 'Exciter' maintains its place in the Top Ten of the greatest metal songs, and would be the template for 'Painkiller' several years down the line when the band tried to rekindle that original fire. It's got everything – speed, excitement, and some finger-knotting guitar leads. It's only weakness, probably as a result of Halford's new rhyming dictionary, was the 'fall to your knees and repent if you please' line which has never been satisfactory; written now, the line would almost certainly be something like 'fall to your knees and repent, mutherfucker.' But then, the Seventies were a little more sedate, even in metal circles.

It's pretty obvious that the band were trying to come up with the fastest song ever written, and it's little wonder that when Diamond Head were aiming to write something fast and furious, it was 'Exciter' that they looked to. ''Exciter'... was a very fast song for the time,' recalled the band's guitarist Brian Tatler in his autobiography, 'and we wrote 'Helpless' not long after hearing it.'

Elaborating later, he explains:

> *I wanted the energy because I always think you've got to play it live, and therefore you've almost certainly got to get it over to a fan who's never heard it before, and the faster songs seemed to work better live. 'Exciter' was the fastest song I knew at the time. That, and Motörhead and a few things like that and also, having thought about it, 'Call For The Priest' – that's a really fast song too. So I think 'Exciter' and 'Call For The Priest' (and 'Victim Of Changes' too, but in a different way), they would have influenced Diamond Head. We probably wanted that fast rhythm, that jackhammer-fast rhythm, and that great metallic guitar sound as well. Diamond Head songs like 'Helpless' and 'Streets Of Gold' definitely owe something to Priest.*

The song would also influence a certain Canadian power trio who ditched their name Hell Razor in favour of Exciter and who would go on to taste success in the early Eighties speed metal boom. It was also a favourite of American band Hellion whose choice of recorded cover versions – including Deep Purple's 'Black Night' and a nice twist on Led Zeppelin's 'Immigrant Song' – shows that they know how to make a song their own without making any radical changes to its familiarity. Vocalist Ann Boleyn had grown up on a diet of Deep Purple and Black Sabbath and discovered *Sad Wings Of Destiny* in 1976.

> *I was completely blown away by how different Judas Priest sounded from*

the other heavy bands at the time. Instead of having one guitarist Priest had two, and they played many of the parts in perfect harmony – kind of like Thin Lizzy, but much more intense. And Rob Halford's vocals were unique: I'd never heard another heavy rock singer hit such high notes.

I had an overnight radio show on KROQ in Los Angeles in the Seventies. One morning the DJ whose shift was after mine arrived quite early. He told me that he'd nearly got a speeding ticket as he was listening to my show in his car when I'd been playing a song by Judas Priest and he put his foot on the gas. He jokingly called my show Speed Metal Hell and that name stuck. To the best of my knowledge, the title of my show was the first time the term 'speed metal' was ever used, so that term which became familiar as the Eighties progressed can be traced right back to Judas Priest and that morning when I was playing them on the airwaves!

'Exciter' became one of those songs we'd mess around with at soundchecks as it was one of our favourites. Hellion had a bit of a chequered career with musicians coming and going, but when some of the original members started asking if they could return we decided to go into the studio and get back to basics. We recorded some songs we'd written earlier but had never had the opportunity to record, and decided to do 'Exciter' just see how it went. We were really pleased with the way it came out. It's such a great song that we decided to keep it as close to the original as possible – there was no need to rework it since Judas Priest's original versions of their songs, both in the studio and on their live recordings, were always excellent.'

'White Heat, Red Hot' (Tipton)

Lyrically, *Stained Class* leapt from sci-fi and fantasy on the one hand, with 'Exciter' becoming one of the many pseudo-comic book champions Halford's imagination would give birth to, to more down-to-earth topics such as the plight of native civilisations being conquered and exploited in 'Savage', ('who's the savage? Modern man…') and the bitter-sweet kiss of fortune and fame in 'Heroes End'. 'Exciter' itself gives way to another future fantasy in 'White Heat, Red Hot'. An up-tempo outing with an interesting drum pattern and an unexpected time change as it nears its conclusion it would also go on to be a stage favourite until, like 'Exciter', it would be culled to make room for *British Steel* material. One of two solo contributions from Tipton, the sci-fi gladiatorial epic possibly inspired the album cover image. Its rousing cry of 'prepare to fight, unsheathe your scythe, a ghastly beam of ill / to slice the life with blinding light and seventh-dimensional skill', revealing a weapon not unlike the light sabre beloved by Jedi Knights in *Star Wars* which of course had been the previous summer's blockbuster movie.

A great album track in its own right, when played live the song was a juggernaut of muscle and blood: think Bruce Banner turning into The Hulk and you'll be in the right ballpark.

'Better By You, Better Than Me' (Gary Wright)

Stained Class was the last album on which CBS in the UK would demand a cover version which could be released as a 'hit single'. The delicious irony here is that when Judas Priest did finally have a hit it was with a self-penned composition as far away from 'Diamonds And Rust' and 'Better By You, Better Than Me' as it's possible to get. But record companies always know best.

So, with the album pretty much finished, the Suits decided that the 'hit single' was still missing and, as such, 'Better By You, Better Than Me' was a late addition to the tracklist. Taped at Utopia Studios in London, the recording was overseen by James Guthrie in the producer's chair as by this time Dennis MacKay was no longer available. The band's take on a track from Spooky Tooth's 1969 release Spooky Two kept fairly closely to the original concept of the song although they tweaked the main riff, beefed up the guitars to compensate for the lack of keyboards, put the foot on the pedal a bit to liven things up and added the 'everybody, everybody knows' bridge. When asked in 2019 by Classic Rock's Dave Everley what he thought of Priest's version, Spooky Tooth's guitarist Luther Grosvenor replied simply: 'Never heard it. I know they had a court case in America over it, something to do with a guy who committed suicide, but I've never bothered to listen to it.'

With fellow album track 'Invader' on the flip the song was released as a single in January 1978; like their Joan Baez cover the previous year, 'Better By You, Better Than Me' would fail to impress record buyers, and the single was one of the many thousands of releases whose existence the chart compilers remained blissfully unaware of. The German pressing came in a natty picture sleeve which features the band looking mean 'n' moody – aside from Halford, that is – in denim and leather, but even that failed to tempt record buyers. What is worth noting though is that during the *Stained Class* sessions the band recorded a version of Gun's 'Race With The Devil' which those loveable metal minxes Girlschool also covered in 1980 and which gave them their first Top 50 single. Just saying…

'Stained Class' (Tipton / Halford)

The album's title cut is possibly one of the band's most under-rated songs, lyrically magnificent and beautifully played throughout with some clever changes in tempo and Halford's voice used to its full advantage. Downing thinks that Halford originally came up with 'Stained Glass' as a possible title, and that it was Tipton who tweaked it. Halford's lyrics for this song are amongst his finest. Although over the years the band have been mocked – and often rightly so – for their dependence on rhyming couplets whatever the cost, here Halford was in his element, delivering the goods in no uncertain style. And the mid-section, where he rolls his tongue around the brutal concoction of syllables 'lethal, deadly / hung, drawn and quartered / He slaughtered and faltered and altered the world / And by doing so smashed all his hopes and utopian dreams…' would come to be a bit of a band trademark, used, for example, in the likes of 'Rapid Fire' and, well, 'Delivering The Goods' to great effect.

Although it wasn't a song that made much impact on Priest's live plans, once Halford had got Fight and Two out of his system and had bounced back with his self-titled band in 2000 'Stained Class' was one of the many oldies to find its way into their set – and boy, did it sound good!

'Invader' (Tipton / Halford / Hill)

'Invader' – Hill's last co-writing credit – closed the original album's first side and is the album's only real weak link. It's not a bad song in its own right but, set against the rest of the material here, it screams 'B-side' and it would probably have been better to have left it off *Stained Class* altogether (and so give the 7" an exclusive non-album flipside) had there been anything else available to take its place. It's a fairly straightforward romp through the alien invasion theme, inspired by, well, take your pick: *Invasion Of the Body Snatchers*, *The Invaders*, *Quatermass 2*, and so on.

'Saints In Hell' (Tipton / Halford / Downing)

In vinyl days you'd flip the record over and be greeted by 'Saints In Hell', a majestic battle between good and evil which redeems its lightweight predecessor. A slow, grinding riff sketches out a song which stretches the vocalist's voice to the limits over the seemingly relentless refrain. With the first pair of verses despatched the song flows from a solid, driving beat to a hacking riff and finally to Halford's glass-shattering refrain. To make things multi-cultural the singer even delivers a line in French, although 'abattoir, abattoir, mon dieu quelle horreur' is bad enough to be a lift from a *Carry On* film.

'Savage' (Downing / Halford)

One of the many revelations in Downing's autobiography is his awareness of being squeezed out by his fellow guitarist, and 'Savage' features one of just three standalone solos he contributes to *Stained Class*. Is it me, or is the guitarist venting his anger through his performance?

'Savage' (as noted previously) brings things back down to earth with its take on colonialism and imperialism as seen from the viewpoint of the conquered and vanquished, who were doing quite well, thank you, until Western Europeans turn up to 'poison my tribe with civilised progress'. On first play, it's seemingly a bit out of place and is the shortest self-penned cut on the album, but it's the song that roots *Stained Class* back in the real world with its unconcealed social conscience.

'Beyond The Realms Of Death' (Binks / Halford)

Still rooted in reality, 'Beyond The Realms Of Death' is possibly the greatest composition Judas Priest have ever written, or will ever write, come to that. It is a song that tells the story of a man who retreats into himself; a song which truly showcases the full range of Halford's lyrical abilities and his incredible voice; a song with a fabulous guitar solo (the envy of so many musicians); a song co-written by a drummer; the undoubted high spot on *Stained Class* and one of the finest six-and-three-quarter-minutes of music committed to tape.

An ambitious composition that calls to mind 'Stairway To Heaven' and which features not only some of Halford's greatest lyrics but also a fabulous solo from Tipton, 'Beyond The Realms Of Death' was co-written by Halford and Binks. It's the only writing credit ever afforded to a drummer on a Judas Priest album and resulted from the left-handed drummer flipping a guitar upside-down and worked out the guitar parts. The gentle opening, the slow build to the chorus, the drop down and build again… It's more a masterclass in songwriting than a song in itself and with Halford wailing like a banshee as the song strides inexorably towards meltdown the rest of the band barely manage to keep the lid on things. And then there's Tipton's solo. 'You can't really pat yourself on the back and say, "I was composing something there that would stand the test of time…"' he told Al King. 'Back in those days we used to go down the pub, have a few pints, come back and jam for a bit and you'd formulate an idea. Some of it is luck – you throw a few things against the wall, some stick, some don't. But it's a solo I'm proud of.' And rightly so. Meanwhile, his partner pulls off the second solo over the song's conclusion, no less important than Tipton's but very much in its shadow.

'Heroes End' (Tipton)

After the showstopper, there has to be an encore. After such a traumatic work-out it would be a crime just to leave things there, and Priest round the album off with 'Heroes End', a song which laments why people have to die to become showbiz heroes ('it's a shame a legend begins at its end'). In focussing on a female singer, a guitarist and a fast-car-lovin' film star it's pretty obvious that Tipton's second solo composition is targeting Janis Joplin, Jimi Hendrix and James Dean. In fairness, it's not the world's greatest song, and if anything is a bit punky in its staccato chorus and poppy in its toe-tapping verse leaving it rather disjointed and an unsatisfactory end to the album. But the song that could actually follow such a towering edifice as 'Beyond The Realms Of Death' has not yet been written by any metal band and almost certainly never will. Again, Tipton unleashes the first solo and Downing lets fly with the second, bringing both the song and *Stained Class* to its conclusion.

Post Album Events

Having tidied away their Christmas presents the five members of Judas Priest – now hardened travellers – packed their bags in January 1978 and set off on the road once more. The *Stained Class* tour commenced on 19 January in West Runton and carried on into the following month when, on 10 February, they headlined Hammersmith Odeon for the first time. It's possibly not a co-incidence that *Stained Class* itself was released that day, the rear cover of the flimsy four-page tour programme carrying a full-page advert for the album. As the tour progressed, so *Stained Class* would go on to peak at No.27 in the UK charts which, at four places lower than *Sin After Sin*, must have been a bit of a disappointment for the band. Across the Atlantic, though, it did break into the

Billboard Top 200 at No.173.

In Heavy Duty Steve Gett pointed out that on previous tours Halford would go through several costume changes during a gig, but this now ceased, with the singer simply dressed in black. Tipton told the author: 'Rob had been through different moods and fashions. We've always tried to cater to what the people expect, and around that time it was a case of being raw and ready, so we just decided to get down to basics'. Or, as Hill notes in the same book: 'It was a tour when we said, 'let's cut the crap and just get out there and play.'

By March the band were back in the US, supporting Foghat, who were a big draw (their 1977 live album had reached No.11 in the American album charts) with big moustaches. 'I don't think they even talked to us,' Tipton told Gett. 'That taught us a lesson, and we've subsequently tried to help support bands in whatever area we can. Foghat weren't helpful at all; apart from not talking to us they only allowed us half-an-hour on stage, and wouldn't even let us use their spotlights.' Terry Dark of fellow Birmingham band Jameson Raid – who as mentioned earlier were coincidentally managed for a while by Priest's former drummer John Hinch – can testify to Priest's attitude to their opening acts. 'When we played with them at Derby, and Sheffield Rob Halford said to me just before we went on, "just go out there and try to blow us off stage. It'll make the whole show better." This was a thousand times better than most bands who were scared to give you a good sound or good monitors and especially not an encore. It's always stuck in my mind, the way he said that.'

Judas Priest's show at the Agora Ballroom in Cleveland on 9 May was recorded, with a few tracks later appearing as B-sides. An on-line setlist for the show runs as follows: 'White Heat, Red Hot' / 'The Ripper' / 'Beyond The Realms Of Death' / 'Victim Of Changes' / 'Starbreaker' / 'Tyrant' / 'Genocide'. If that isn't one of the greatest sets by a support band ever, then what is?

From America, the boys went on to their first visit to Japan, where – like so many other acts – they experienced their own version of Beatlemania everywhere they went. The band played five shows (three in Tokyo, one in Nagoya and the final night on 5 August in Osaka) after which they were soon on a plane bound for home and then, incredibly, back in the studio to start work on Album Number Five which was in the shops – in the UK at least – by October. No pressure, then…

Killing Machine (1978)

Personnel:
Robert Halford: lead vocals
Glenn Tipton: lead guitars
K.K. Downing: lead guitars
Ian Hill: bass
Les Binks: drums
Record label: CBS
Recorded at Utopia, Basing Street and CBS Studios, London, August/September 1978
Produced by: Dennis MacKay, co-produced by Judas Priest
Release date: 9 October 1978 / February 1979 (as *Hell Bent For Leather*)
Highest chart positions: UK: 32, US: 128 (as *Hell Bent For Leather*)
Running time: 35:06 / 38:30 (as *Hell Bent For Leather*)

> *I have to be honest; I laughed my tits off when I saw them on* Top Of The Pops – Al Atkins

Killing Machine, Judas Priest's second album release of 1978, was the final piece in the jigsaw that promoted the band from what was then the second division of metal's league tables to the first, or from cult to mainstream. At the seventh attempt, the band finally had a hit single – and major labels just love hit singles! – in 'Take On The World', a slice of power pop taken from the elegantly and enigmatically sleeved album which, furthermore, was the first of the band's LPs to be issued in coloured vinyl (fittingly a bright, blood red). But perhaps more importantly, *Killing Machine* boasted neither an epic ballad like 'Victim Of Changes' or 'Beyond The Realms Of Death' nor a frenetic 'Sinner'-style workout. This time around the settled line-up of Rob Halford, Glenn Tipton, K.K. Downing, Ian Hill and Les Binks served up ten short, snappy bursts of metal – eleven on the alternatively-named US version – with not one song longer than four-and-a-quarter minutes and a trio of cuts done and dusted in less than three. As Satan's Russ Tippins points out:

> *It's hard to second-guess why they did this, but from the outside looking in it certainly looked more like a conscious decision to go for a complete change of image and approach to songwriting rather than a natural or subliminal progression. From* Stained Class *to* Killing Machine *is quite a leap, possibly the biggest single leap of their career. The three albums* Sad Wings Of Destiny, Sin After Sin *and* Stained Class *are all very similar in that they feature those great, epic, lengthy, exciting songs. They're not written to what you'd call formulaic arrangements. But that's exactly what they started doing on* Killing Machine; *they started writing to the verse-chorus-verse-chorus formula and as a result, started to sound more, well, poppy. At the same time, that's when the leather and chains started coming into the equation as well. Up to that point they had been quite hippy-ish really,*

> *jeans and cheesecloth shirts, that kind of thing, a bit like the old Sabbath image, if 'image' is even the right word. Somewhere along the line, they made a conscious decision that the songs were going to be shorter and catchier and that they'd have that leather and studs biker image to go with it. It got them into the singles charts, no denying that, but the songs weren't as interesting as they were on those earlier albums.*

On its release in October 1978, in purely commercial terms *Killing Machine* itself was a bit of a disappointment for CBS, failing to stop the slide in chart success and peaking just outside the Top 30 at No.32, five places below its predecessor (although its tenure in the charts was almost twice as long, evidence of greater long-term sales). But as an artistic statement, it was an album fit for its time. No doubt the songwriters were aware that in a country awash with punk and phlegm songs were now by and large being kept short and to the point, and despite not displaying the complexity and virtuosity of their previous albums the ten songs on offer were still exciting and easily accessible. And then there was the sound. 'On *Killing Machine* the sound that they would develop on later albums with producer Tom Allom starts to become apparent,' points out Soldier's guitarist Miles Goodman. 'It's the first album really in which a more powerful production in the sense of grittier sound is employed to maximum effect, and it's the experimental nature of all the previous albums that finally brings us to this: a fully realised band that's found its niche.' The other big change was in the lyrical content department. Gone was the sci-fi of *Stained Class* to be replaced by more gritty imagery centred either on real life or sexual fantasy. The cover reflected this change, too, with Roslaw Szaybo turning in another image, although this time a rather disturbing dystopian visage wearing blood-red shattered goggles.

James Guthrie, the producer who'd impressed the band on the late addition to *Stained Class*, was chosen to helm the new Judas Priest LP, and turned in a masterpiece of metal that became one of the albums that served if not as a precursor then a gateway to what was to become known as the New Wave Of British Heavy Metal. And the biker image that Judas Priest and particularly Rob Halford adopted became almost *de rigeur* for the new up-and-coming NWOBHM bands.

With their new-look leather and studs image, Judas Priest did present an arresting appearance to link in with an album that was as obnoxious and in-your-face as the punk bands that were selling out venues across the UK. *Killing Machine* offers up four very metal cuts punctuated by one ballad on each side of the original LP. There's little breathing space, little room to move; *Killing Machine* forces you into a corner from which there is no way out. It was a brave and bold step and one which no doubt cost the band some fans. There's nothing particularly subtle or intricate or progressive about 'Running Wild' or 'Hell Bent For Leather', and 'Evil Fantasies' is as genitally-fixated as you can get, but you can't make an omelette without breaking eggs, and the band obviously felt it was time to move on.

As if finally having some faith in the band, CBS released four singles off *Killing Machine*. September 1978's edit of 'Evening Star' (coupled with a live version of 'Starbreaker') preceded the album but failed to shine, and October's pairing of album cuts 'Before The Dawn' b/w 'Rock Forever' continued the trend of not bothering the single charts in the slightest. After two complete flops, you'd have thought the record company would have given the band some cash and told them to go on tour and come back in a year's time with another record, preferably one with a single on it. But instead, something strange happened. Veering from the obvious chart-friendly material on the album in January 1979 CBS threw the anthemic 'Take On The World' at the record-buying public and watched – probably in complete befuddlement – as it climbed the singles charts and peaked at No.14, terrorising people in their own homes as they tuned into *Top Of The Pops* on 25 January. Maybe the marketing men had got it right this time, as they seemed to have pulled out all the stops for 'Take On The World'. The band's first single available as both a 7" and 12" featured their first picture sleeve (a striking black and white shot of Halford) and came backed with two cuts recorded at the Agora Ballroom, Cleveland, the previous May. These were 'White Heat, Red Hot' and 'Starbreaker' (the same version that had already backed 'Evening Star'), although just the latter cut completed the 7" single.

Realising that if something's worth doing, it's probably worth doing twice, 'Evening Star' was re-issued in May, this time as a clear vinyl 12" with another live song from Cleveland 'Beyond The Realms Of Death' and the studio version of the cover of Fleetwood Mac's 'The Green Manalishi (With The Two-Pronged Crown)'. And although the single's progress stuttered to a halt just outside the Top 50, Judas Priest had finally got the taste for writing hit singles, and for appearing on *Top Of The Pops*, come to that, as they made their second appearance in front of the teeny-bopping audience on 17 May. Things would probably never be quite the same again.

Yet every silver lining is enveloped by a cloud, and despite the band's credible performance on the show a lot of their hardcore fans weren't happy at seeing the object of their devotion prancing around on *Top Of The Pops* like metal marionettes. The letters page in *Sounds* carried some interesting correspondence in the weeks following the 'Take On The World' performance, and Geoff Barton would later make a significant chunk of his *Unleashed In The East* review an open letter with which to remonstrate with disgruntled fans.

Possibly to put some space between it and *Stained Class* and/or to tie in better with the year's first batch of US dates *Killing Machine* wasn't released in the States until February 1979. In fact, technically it wasn't released at all. It's baffling to Europeans that a nation that's so liberal with gun control can be so squeamish when it comes to anything that veers towards a depiction of violence, but the powers-that-be decided that the album couldn't go out under such a title and demanded it be re-named. So, with a bit of judicious air-brushing of the cover and one change of title track later, *Hell Bent For Leather* appeared in American shops a full four months after its original release. This 'new' album boasted an extra song too, with the studio version of 'The Green Manalishi (With The Two-Pronged Crown)' – the track which backed the second UK single release of 'Evening Star' – squeezed in on Side Two between 'Burning Up' and the original title cut. Arguably this was done because it gave the label 'radio airplay options' and was indeed released as a single in the States, with 'Rock Forever' on the flip, although failed to make any impression. Cynics, however, would argue that the addition of 'The Green Manalishi' meant that US fans who'd splashed out a lot of money for an import copy of *Killing Machine* would now be able to get a domestic version too. Meanwhile, in the UK completists would want to scour the import shops to hunt down and pick up the US album for a bonus track and a hefty price. If there's one thing record companies like more than selling one copy of an album, it's selling two copies. Ker-ching all round!

'Delivering The Goods' (Tipton / Downing / Halford)

With its brief but slightly off-kilter intro throwing a bit of a swerveball before crashing into business, 'Delivering The Goods' sets out the album's stall with minimum fuss and maximum metal. In fact, it takes just fourteen seconds for the false, friendly opening to turn nasty and bite the hand that feeds. Lyrically it's no great shakes, the band hitting the stage wrapped up with a smattering of nudge-nudge innuendo, but it's an aggressive and cocky opener and in the deliciously banal 'we don't pull no punches / we aim where the crunch is' Halford delivers one of his finest throwaway couplets ever. Everything is trimmed to avoid excess fat so the guitar solo is short and snappy, although Halford's vocals soar and Binks – yes, he's still there, the first drummer to play on two consecutive records – handles proceedings with little fuss. This is no 'Exciter'-style work-out, although he does get to flex his muscles at the end of the song. At four-and-a-quarter minutes, 'Delivering The Goods' is *Killing Machine*'s longest track, which shows that the band had certainly undergone a radical rethink in the songwriting department.

'Rock Forever' (Tipton / Downing / Halford)

A huge chunk of *Killing Machine* went straight into Priest's live set and, like 'Delivering The Goods', the rather silly 'Rock Forever' – a paean to rock music as the antidote to a bad day; a similar idea (but worse) would appear on *Point Of Entry* under the title of 'Hot Rockin'' – would also make the cut. This fairly lightweight – almost throwaway – ode to the joys of rockin' out with, again, a clipped solo and a short running time which just about limps over the three-minute mark is, to be brutally honest, not the best three minutes of anyone's time.

'Evening Star' (Tipton / Halford)

Things gear down for this catchy piece of power-pop which in edited form would be issued twice as a single, dying a death in September 1978 as the album's taster and being marginally more successful in April 1979 (hitting No.53) as the last 45 to be taken from the album. The single edit hacked out the second part of the solo and the third verse rather brutally, but it did get them back on *Top Of the Pops*. Although there's nothing overt in the lyrics – at no point does Halford sing in a broad Brummie accent 'oh look, there's the baby Jesus!' – some commentators have speculated that the song is about the journey of the Biblical Magi to Bethlehem, led by the evening star of the title and that, as the narrator, Halford is either Melchior, Caspar or Balthazar. Or it could be about a particularly memorable 18-30s holiday. It's soulfully delivered though, and a pleasant enough way to greet the middle of the LP's first side.

'Hell Bent For Leather' (Tipton)

A perennial live favourite which vanishes as quickly as the lyric's character, a mysterious biker who's 'black as night / faster than a shadow' and whose challengers 'died as they tried' to take him on. A curiously likeable piece of hokum in a blink-and-you'll-miss-it kind of way (it's all over in two-and-a-half minutes), the concept was revisited in 'Machine Man' on the Ripper Owens-era *Demolition* and in a way is a precursor to 'Breaking The Law'. It's a fast, no-frills workout, written to capture a bike at speed, and a much better way to show how a short song can still be versatile and stylish: it also features the album's second-star rhyme in 'an exhibition / of sheer precision'.

'Take On The World' (Tipton / Halford)

Who'd have thought that this mid-paced and clichéd clunker – a blatant stab at copying Queen's October 1977 'We Are The Champions' / 'We Will Rock You' double A-side single in one go – with its hackneyed lyrics and lack of solo would finally give the band the hit single everyone seemed to clamour for? The middle eight gives Halford a chance to flex his vocal cords, but otherwise, it's duh-duh-duh-duh-duh-duh-duh-duh / duh-duh-duh-duh-duh-duh-duh-duh all the way to the end. Although the band actually would later use a drum machine, you do wonder if Binks must have been thinking about what to have for tea as he mindlessly beat out the rhythm. But there is a moral here: next time you're in a meeting and afraid to share your ideas for being ridiculed, remember that someone once timidly said 'well, we could always release 'Take On the World' as a single.'

Perhaps even more bizarrely, The Human League covered the song. 'The first gig [after the original split] was at Doncaster Rotters, and the response seemed to be good,' the band's Ian Burden revealed in Mojo. 'Philip [Oakley] and Adrian [Wright] stood on top of a tower and did Judas Priest's 'Take On The World' as the opening number. I was so focused on all these switches and knobs and sliders that I didn't pay much attention really.'

To be fair, 'Take On The World' is actually quite a stylish stomp and closes the side with volume, cartoon violence and the crash of a gong. And you don't get to say that very often.

'Burnin' Up' (Downing / Tipton)

Although somewhere along the line the Priest mythology had the band targeted for sexual content, this was the first time Halford really dipped his toes (or anything else) into the pool of steamy sex, and yet he didn't even write it. The sexy 'n' sassy 'Burnin' Up' is one of the band's forgotten gems. It never made the live set (although a few seconds of the synth intro did open the shows) but is an off-beat and likeable outing, and once you get past the second chorus charged eroticism and a forceful guitar break unleash the band beautifully.

'Killing Machine' (Tipton)

Another lost gem, another song that should have made the live set, this quirky little story about a hitman is perhaps an odd choice for the title track. Again, the solo is kept to a minimum as the song just makes it to the three-minute mark, although along with 'Burnin' Up' 'Killing Machine' is perhaps the closest the album gets to old-school Judas Priest. Both songs hark back to a more progressive way of working, and the shady world evoked by the contract killer lyrics certainly fits with the seeming uncertainty and edginess of the music.

'Running Wild' (Tipton)

No pause for breath as yet another short and spirited Tipton solo composition leaps out of nowhere and considerably ups the tempo once more. Like 'Hell Bent For Leather' on the other side of the record 'Running Wild' became a stage favourite and again words and music gel on the story of a larger-than-life character who lives his life his way. It's another attention-grabbing song that caused a young band to sit down, have a re-think and change their name, as German singer/guitarist Rock 'n' Rolf (or Rolf Kasparek to his mum) explains:

> *This was around 1979 when the live record came out. We needed to change the name of the band from Granite Hearts because some of the guys had left, and one of the guys in the band came up with Running Wild because we were all great Judas Priest fans at that time. I discovered the band myself around 1978. There was this TV show in Germany, and they performed 'Rock Forever', and I really liked the song and tried to get the record. But as I couldn't find it I bought* Sin After Sin *instead. That's a really great album, and I really became a big fan of the band. After that, I bought the second one and the first one, any records I could get, in fact.*
>
> *Judas Priest were a big influence. In the first line-up of Running Wild everybody was a big Judas Priest fan; so naturally, we really tried to sound like Judas Priest and to write songs like Judas Priest, even though we weren't good enough to do it! But we played around with the sound and tried to create our own style a bit; and we really loved their look, which is why we had leather and studs and stuff like that when we first started out because we were really impressed by that. To us, it meant real heavy metal. It summed everything up that was real metal to me at that time – their attitude, their aggressiveness and the look and the sound.*

'Before The Dawn' (Downing / Tipton / Halford)

The token ballad (and failed single) finally makes an appearance towards the end of the album. A rather quaint yet tender affair with some touching lyrics, the acoustic outing is both beautifully written and beautifully executed and rather enlivened by Downing's solo, although he notes in his autobiography that his finger-flexing was supposed to be longer:

> *As a guitarist, when presented with great chord changes, there's so much room to create great solos. So, you can imagine what the solo was originally like. Glenn though, somehow thinking that 'Before The Dawn' might be a potential single, moved to have my solo radically cut down. In my eyes, it was only because the song was entirely my composition that he let me do the solo at all!*

'Evil Fantasies' (Tipton / Halford / Downing)

More sweaty sex! With 'Evil Fantasies' Halford starts to nudge the band near to the S&M territory for which they would later become (incorrectly) infamous. It's a tongue-in-cheek romp which works well as an album closer: a bit like bad sex, at its conclusion it does liven up a bit, but it takes a long time to get there and you have to wonder if it was actually worth it. No great solo, just a few licks here and there to accompany Halford's orgiastic exclamations, and then take him to the fade. And presumably the post-coital cigarette. The song works much better live, as the B-side to 'Living After Midnight' was to prove.

'The Green Manalishi (With The Two-Pronged Crown)' (Peter Green)

If you're used to the UK running order, the intrusion of this Fleetwood Mac cover is a tad unwelcome. Released on the second outing of the 'Evening Star' single on this side of the Atlantic and squeezed onto the second side of the LP between 'Burnin' Up' and 'Killing Machine' for the US *Hell Bent For Leather* album 'The Green Manalishi (With The Two-Pronged Crown') is another song that would carve a place for itself in the band's set for eternity. Priest upped the tempo of the original quite considerably – the original version is a bit of a dirge – and cut away anything extraneous that detracted from their new-found short and direct approach, lopping a minute off the running time. If you're going to do a cover version, make it your own, and that's exactly what Priest did here, leading many later fans to believe it was a self-penned composition. It's apparently a song about the evils of money, written by Peter Green who famously gave a lot of his away: a manalishi is also a term for someone with a lot of cash who likes to flash it around. Apparently…

Post Album Events

Bizarrely, the review in *Sounds*, penned by Pete Silverton, gave the album just one star. Under the heading 'As Butch As A Bubble Bath,' the reviewer made his disdain abundantly clear, noting that, for example:

> *'Evil Fantasies' could be any one of a number of Zeppelin tracks, 'Kashmir' comes to mind immediately, but it possesses neither the blockheaded rush nor the dynamic range of its spiritual mentor, while 'Before The Dawn' is hippy-dippism, the romance that normally dare not speak its name outside the confines of a Mills & Boon novel … Queen get their chance on 'Take On The World', an obvious first cousin to 'We Will Rock You'. And nowhere do Priest realise – unlike Blue Oyster Cult at their best – that if you wanna pretend you're a morbid, sexually perverted creep, it's a good idea to make fun of yourself… Fortunately, that ludicrous title [referring to the LP itself] is nothing but pubescent bombast.*

Although that was not what the band wanted to read – where was Geoff Barton when they needed him? – the open road beckoned once more. As the album started to appear in the racks Judas Priest stopped by at the BBC for an In Concert recording on 23 October 1978 where they ran through 'White Heat, Red Hot', 'Victim Of Changes', 'Beyond The Realms Of Death', newbie 'Running Wild' and 'Starbreaker'. It's an interesting set in its own right (whether anything else remains in the vaults aside from the 30 minutes that were broadcast is one for the archivists), but on the night the band sound almost forced and quite uncomfortable for the first couple of songs. Things loosen up though, and by the time 'Beyond The Realms Of Death' gets into gear the band are at the top of their game once more.

The X Certificate tour (as the 1978 UK dates were dubbed) kicked off properly the following night at Blackburn and drew to a conclusion at Peterborough Wirrina Stadium on 24 November where the set was: 'Exciter' / 'White Heat, Red Hot' / 'Sinner' / 'Killing Machine'/'Rock Forever' / 'Beyond The Realms Of Death' / 'Running Wild' / 'Evil Fantasies' / 'Delivering The Goods' / ''Victim Of Changes' / 'Starbreaker' / 'Genocide'.

After a well-earned break – 1978 had been one hell of a busy year – and having packed away the decorations and worked off the Christmas pud (and got their debut *Top Of The Pops* appearance out of the way as well) in February 1979 they found themselves back in Japan once more to start the opening leg of the now officially christened *Killing Machine* tour. After the Japanese dates, some of which were taped for a live album, Judas Priest flew to the US for a tour that would keep them on the road until 6 May supporting the likes of Pat Travers and UFO. When that tour finished, they came home and spent the rest of the month crisscrossing the UK (again), with Marseille in tow (tickets £2.50, £3.00 on the door).

Presumably, to capitalise on the UK dates, this was when 'Evening Star' was re-issued and gave the band their second *Top Of The Pops* performance. Unfortunately, they gave the 'sell-out' naysayers plenty more ammunition: the day of filming coincided with the first of two hometown gigs at Birmingham Odeon, and as a consequence of going to London, the band arrived back at the Odeon horrendously late. In terms of own goals putting *Top Of The Pops* above your home crowd is about as heinous a crime as a band can commit. Fortunately, it's not the sort of thing you do twice…

Somewhere along the line, as the UK leg of the tour drew to a close, so did Les Binks' tenure with the band, the drummer playing his last date on 31 May 1979. Golden Rule #1: it's never a good idea to get too comfy on the Judas Priest drum stool.

There's never really been a satisfactory explanation as to why Binks left the band. In *Sounds* in particular at the time, he was often referred to as Les 'Feathertouch' Binks, but his contribution to *Stained Class* has been emphasised time and time again, and he certainly handled 'Exciter' with the pace and verve the song demands. The only thing commentators seem to agree on is that he was a vegetarian, and Judas Priest were a band of carnivores. His replacement, Dave Holland, would have been well known to the rest of the band, having been born in Wolverhampton and worked around the West Midlands. There he eventually found fame as the drummer in Trapeze, the band that also featured Glenn Hughes (who would leave in 1973 to join Deep Purple) and Mel Galley who would later pop up in Whitesnake. Holland joined Judas Priest in August, and after learning the set was soon on a plane to America with the rest of the band where dates commenced on 1 September, supporting Kiss for a month and then playing selective headline shows – no pressure on the new boy, then! The Kiss support slot is a Priest feast in itself, this set captured at the Municipal Auditorium, Kansas City, 30 September: 'Hell Bent For Leather' / 'Delivering The Goods' / 'The Ripper' / 'Running Wild' / 'Diamonds And Rust' / 'Victim Of Changes' / 'The Green Manalishi (With The Two-Pronged Crown)' / Starbreaker' / 'Tyrant'. The show a few days previously on 24 September in Milwaukee – the home of the Harley Davidson – marked the motorbike's onstage debut. At this time the company was going through lean times and the original bike was bought for one dollar on the strength of the advertising it would hopefully gain the company as the band toured the world.

A stunning show (captured on a bootleg entitled *The Ripper*) at The Palladium, New York on 4 November was a fitting climax to a very successful tour of America. A few days later the band were back to Europe where they supported AC/DC across the continent on a tour which kept them busy until 15 December. Then, after the second of two nights in Nice, they packed their bags, did their Christmas shopping in the Duty-Free and came home for a bit of tinsel and turkey, reflecting on what a successful year 1979 had been.

Unleashed In The East (1979)

Personnel:
Rob Halford: vocals
Glenn Tipton: lead guitars
K.K. Downing: lead guitars
Ian Hill: bass
Les Binks: drums
Record label: CBS
Recorded live at Kosei Nenkin Hall, Tokyo, and Nakano Sunplaza, Tokyo, on 10 and 15 February 1979
Produced by: Tom Allom and Judas Priest
Release date: 17 September 1979
Highest chart positions: UK: 10, US: 70
Running time: 44:35 (free three-track EP 13:42)

> ***An album that I've heard people refer to as the best heavy metal live album of all time*** – K.K. Downing, *Heavy Duty*

To Geoff Barton in *Sounds,* it was 'one of the finest HM albums I've heard all year, and if you don't buy it because you objected to 'Take On The World', you should be shot at dawn. You'll be missing out on perhaps the third greatest live album of all time…'

To Steve Gett in *Melody Maker*, it was 'an anthology of the greatest hits of Judas Priest to date in concert … An excellent representation of the band's on-stage capabilities ... Compulsive buying for all devotees of heavy metal…'

To Rob Halford, K.K. Downing, Glenn Tipton, Ian Hill and Les Binks it was Judas Priest's first Top 10 LP.

To the rest of us at home, it was simply *Unleashed In The East*.

As mentioned in the previous chapter, February 1979 saw Judas Priest back in Japan, where they played six gigs, opening with two nights at Tokyo's Kosei Nenkin Hall on 9 and 10 February. This latter date had both a 4pm and 7pm show, followed by two nights at the Festival Hall, Osaka (13 and 14 February) and then back to Tokyo for one more night at the Nakano Sunplaza. Two Tokyo concerts, the evening show on 10 February and the final night at Nakano Sunplaza gig on 15 February, were officially recorded to provide material for the band's first and best live album.

The old adage says that if something is too good to be true then it probably is, but the setlist for the tour was a true fan's delight, a mouth-watering array of songs that even today leaves the rest of the world as green as a manalishi with envy: 'Exciter' / 'Running Wild' / 'The Ripper' / 'Diamonds And Rust' / 'Rock Forever' / 'Beyond The Realms Of Death' / 'The Green Manalishi (With The Two-Pronged Crown)' / 'Delivering The Goods' / 'White Heat, Red Hot' / 'Sinner' / 'Evil Fantasies' / 'Victim Of Changes' / 'Genocide' / 'Starbreaker' / 'Hell Bent For Leather' / 'Take On The World' / 'Tyrant'.

Live albums are notoriously tricky; it's hard to satisfy everyone because some people want raw grittiness, while others want perfection with applause. Some fans (and bands) like their live albums to be a valid representation of what happened on the night (or nights) and if there's a bum note or two, so what? For other fans (and bands) though, the live album has to be spot-on. The bum note that whizzed by on the night has now been captured on tape for all time, and that's something some musicians just can't live with.

So, as everyone knows, *Unleashed In The East* was overdubbed, but then, countless live albums have been manipulated in some way or another. Running Wild's Rock 'n' Rolf is a huge fan of *Unleashed In The East*, and he probably sums it up for 99.9% of fans. 'That live record was great; the sound of the guitars is really amazing and was another thing that had a real impact on us as a band. We really wanted our guitars to sound that kind of way, that heavy, that distorted; that was something we really tried to copy.' But the tales of the album being overdubbed do nothing to spoil his enjoyment of it. 'Why should they?' he laughs. 'Everybody does it.'

Once the UK leg of the tour was over in the summer of 1979, the tapes of the two Japanese shows were taken to Startling Studios to be mixed by producer Tom Allom. Although this was the first time the band had worked with Allom, he would go on to become the band's long-term collaborator and produce every future album until 1990's *Painkiller* and was then reunited with them for 2009's *A Touch Of Evil Live* album. Ironically, one of Allom's earliest credits was as engineer on the first few Black Sabbath albums, working alongside early Judas Priest producer Rodger Bain. But in the summer of 1979, his job was to mix and produce the top cuts from the two nights of recordings and come up with an exciting and cohesive single live LP. However, tongues began to wag when Halford was seen at Startling, headphones on, singing away as happy as a pig in poo. Surely he wasn't overdubbing the vocals, was he? First came the denials, then slight admissions that the album had been overdubbed, but no-one seemed to be telling the same story. Tipton is on record as saying that Halford had a cold and needed to touch up some vocal lines; Allom recalled that they needed to patch up some guitar work.

All that aside, the real issue with the album isn't how much overdubbing was carried out, but why the material was cut and pasted to fit a single 40 minute LP when it could have been the last great live album of the Seventies. It should have been a double live set wrapped in an opulent gatefold sleeve boasting a blizzard of live shots from the tour. To compound the disappointment, the front and rear cover shots are so obviously staged that it's little wonder that allegations of studio shenanigans were soon doing the rounds. You would have thought that if a band was going to record a live album, they'd have had someone on hand to shoot a handful of stills for the cover, but the images for *Unleashed In The East* were mocked up at the famous Dunstable Civic Hall (since demolished and replaced by an Asda supermarket) by photographer Fin Costello, giving rise to a tongue-in-cheek title of *Unleashed In The East Of The*

Chilterns. To make matters worse, if worse they could be, both the cover of 2007's *Classic Rock Presents Heavy Metal* and Steve Gett's 1979 *Melody Maker* review carried alternative photos from the session, both of which are better than the two which adorned the album sleeve. (The shot on the magazine cover was also used on the *Concert Classics* is-it-official-or-is-it-a-bootleg release of 1998.) And to overcome the problem that Binks played on the album but was no longer a member of the band by the summer of 1979, the vacant drum kit was neatly obscured in every shot by poses struck by the vocalist.

But what of it? Compared to the legendary and possible overtly-indulgent live albums of the early Seventies, *Unleashed In The East* is not exactly a pedigree pooch, but mongrels are just as attentive and as much fun to play with as thoroughbreds. As Dutch guitarist Willem Verbuyst of Vanderbuyst puts it, 'every time I play this record, and that first riff kicks off, I think 'damn, I wish I'd been there,' and that thought never leaves me throughout the album. Of course, the critics will tell you that it's not really 'live', and dismiss it as Unleashed In The Studio – a discussion reminiscent of Thin Lizzy's *Live And Dangerous*. But does it really matter? I dare to say it doesn't. Certainly, it didn't to the fans as it became one of their best-selling albums, and for me, it is a very credible live album, definitely a lot more 'live' than some contemporary bands with their endless onstage backing tracks. The live energy encapsulated on *Unleashed In The East* is breath-taking, and some of the tracks are really, really heavy. The rendition of 'Victim Of Changes' is smoking and their brave interpretation of Peter Green's 'The Green Manalishi' sounds like it was written by the band themselves, it fits so well into their repertoire. *Unleashed In The East* is a killer record, the kind of album that's a hard rock musician's dream.'

Like the fans, the press loved *Unleashed In The East*. 'Exciter' from the *Stained Class* album opens the show, generating more speed and vitality than the studio version, and featuring electrifying solo work from guitarists K.K. Downing and Glenn Tipton. The drama and momentum are maintained by 'Running Wild', and by the end of this second cut, one has already lost count of the riffs and lead breaks. Sheer proof that Judas Priest, whose third album *Sin After Sin* might have more aptly been titled 'Riff After Riff' make the sort of music which has rendered bands like Black Sabbath redundant. The Sabs just couldn't compete…' reckoned Steve Gett in *Melody Maker*. Over in *Sounds*, Geoff Barton was no less enthusiastic, his five-star review more than making up for the drubbing his colleague Pete Silverton had previously handed out to *Killing Machine*:

> *It's blistering, breathless excitement all the way through from 'Exciter', (taken at about twice the speed of the studio original) to 'Tyrant' and if events temporarily go from brilliant down to so-so on track one, Side Two (with Joan Baez's 'Diamonds And Rust', not my favourite of Priest tracks with those lines about scrappy hotel rooms in Washington Square seeming out of place in the midst of all the other numbers' apocalyptic*

> *fury) that's forgivable, it's the only real mistake that the band make. My favourite moments are 'Green Manalishi' (the Peter Green original hacked to death in gloriously gory fashion), 'Running Wild' (short but supreme) and 'Genocide' (the flashing senseless sabres scythe out of your speakers and leave the cloth coverings hanging torn and tattered). But there are so many fine snatches to be found in 'Sinner', 'Ripper' (listen for singer Rob Halford trying to talk Cockney during the 'I'm a nasty surprise…' verse… CBS should really release this as a single, or would that be a touch too gruesome in the light of the current goings-on in the Yorkshire environs?) and 'Victim Of Changes' (the all-time Priest classic given titanic treatment) as well it seems harsh to give specific tracks particular distinction. The EP contains 'Rock Forever', 'Hell Bent For Leather' and another version of 'Beyond The Realms Of Death' [the review commented earlier on the Agora Ballroom version on the B-side to 'Evening Star'] to round things out nicely, and although it's a pity that there's no 'Evil Fantasies' you can't have everything I suppose.*

The *Sounds*' scribe's wish was soon to come true, as the B-side of the band's next single 'Living After Midnight', released as a taster for *British Steel* in March 1980, carried a further two live cuts from the Tokyo gigs – an emasculated version of 'Delivering The Goods' and an extremely hot rendition of Barton's beloved 'Evil Fantasies'.

Meanwhile, as mentioned in the review, the first pressing of *Unleashed In The East* came with a 7" single with three bonus tracks, the two short 'n' snappy numbers from *Killing Machine* and the finest live version of 'Beyond The Realms Of Death' ever recorded (which, quite bizarrely, has never been issued on CD). The Japanese LP *Priest In The East* came with a four-track EP boasting 'Hell Bent For Leather' and 'Rock Forever', 'Delivering The Goods' (the complete version with the introduction, removed from the UK B-side release, fully intact) and 'Starbreaker'. The three-track EP with the British pressing was, incidentally, later released as a 12" single in The Netherlands. The Dutch also had a single pulled from the album, with the live version of 'Diamonds And Rust' (in a picture sleeve – a production of the album cover) backed by 'Rock Forever'. A US 7" twinned 'Diamonds And Rust' with the *Priest In The East* version of 'Starbreaker'.

Many fans hoped that when *Unleashed In The East* was revisited as part of the 2001 re-issues series, it would be spruced up with all the missing tracks from the gig and maybe even put into the original on-the-night running order. In fact, it was a straight lift from the *Priest In The East* CD, and when the four bonus tracks were touted as never before being available on CD, someone was being a tad untruthful. But at least the bulk of the show was now available without paying import prices; just 'White Heat Red Hot' and 'Take On The World' remain unaccounted for, and, as mentioned before, 'Beyond The Realms Of Death' has yet to debut officially on CD.

Meanwhile, in his conclusion to his review of *Unleashed in The East*, Steve

Gett noted: 'It'll be interesting to see how Priest fare with their next album, for in the confines of the recording studio they have yet to make their full impact.'

Devotees didn't have to wait long to find out. In the meantime, CBS re-isued *Sin After Sin, Stained Class* and *Killing Machine* as a tasty budget-price box set, just to keep things ticking over.

British Steel (1980)

Personnel:
Rob Halford: vocals
Glenn Tipton: lead guitars
K.K. Downing: lead guitars
Ian Hill: bass
Dave Holland: drums
Record label: CBS
Recorded at: Startling Studios, Ascot, January – February 1980
Produced by: Tom Allom
Release date: 14 April 1980
Highest chart positions: UK: 4, US: 34
Running time: 36:10

> *There's nothing on the album I don't like. I like every song, but if I had to pick one favourite it would have to be 'Breaking The Law'* – Rock 'n' Rolf, Running Wild

Everyone knows the stories by now. The swooshing pool cues, the clanking trays of tableware, the broken bottles and Rob Halford, lying awake at night unable to get Glenn Tipton out of his mind as the guitarist noodled away after midnight in a room below the singer's and between them the pair coming up with the band's biggest hit single. From such stories are legends born.

British Steel is the album that sprang Higgs Bosun-like from the head-on collision between the more idealised, progressive metal of *Sin After Sin* and *Stained Class* and the shorter, punkier, formulaic four-fours of *Killing Machine*. It's not the band's best album by any stretch of the imagination, but it is probably the fans' favourite. In Planet Rock magazine's 'The Buyers Guide' feature on Priest, *British Steel* sat at the top of their Top 10 countdown, and if someone says they only own one of the band's albums, it's a safe bet it's this one. It contains some of the fastest, heaviest material they'd ever written, yet also spawned three hit singles – two of which just failed to break into the UK Top Ten – and in doing so catapulted them hilariously into the video age. It was also their first truly trans-Atlantic album, not only peaking at No. 4 in the UK chart on its release in April but also giving the band their first US Top 100, placing at No. 34. It became their first US platinum album in the process, so it's perhaps no great surprise that when they announced for its thirtieth anniversary that they would be playing *British Steel* in its entirety, this set was only toured in America. At least it was captured for posterity on the *British Steel* – 30th Anniversary Deluxe package which featured both audio and visual recordings of the band at the Seminole Hard Rock Arena, Hollywood, Florida on August 17 2009. And *British Steel* also introduced to the world another new drummer in Dave Holland – the fifth person to occupy the drum stool since the band first got a record deal and the eighth since Al Atkins originally decided to paint the name 'Judas Priest' on the front of a bass drum skin.

Yet despite the fact that they could have toured the album to death in America thanks to the groundwork they'd laid in the previous years ,the band were off the road by mid-August. Within a handful of months of *British Steel*'s release Judas Priest were already concentrating on a new record, the mistake only realised when the critically acclaimed, but seemingly terribly rushed and totally unsatisfying *Point Of Entry* failed to please the fanbase. It appeared – for a while at least – that maybe, just maybe, with *British Steel* Judas Priest had peaked and were on the way back down already.

There's also a strange irony that although the *British Steel* world tour kicked off in the UK in March 1980, the band didn't actually play anything from the album on those dates, relying instead on the *Unleashed In The East* set , although by the time the tour reached America four new songs had been integrated. The irony is compounded in that, for the almost unforgivable second time, the start of a hometown gig was delayed because the band were recording yet another performance for *Top Of The Pops*. Even though they weren't even playing the song on stage at this point in time, Priest were whisked down to London to film another mimed studio routine for *British Steel*'s first single 'Living After Midnight' on the day of a gig at Birmingham Odeon. Their seeming preference for success in the singles charts over the loyalty of their hometown fans did no doubt damage their reputation. Again. Shooting themselves in one foot in May 1979 was one thing, but then doing it all over again in front of the same crowd less than a year later was for some people the final straw. Diamond Head's Brian Tatler remembers the occasion well:

> *Everybody was hanging about wanting to see Priest, all excited, but of course, we were all conscious that we had to catch the last bus home. So you did keep checking your watch thinking, 'Bloody hell! Hurry up!' because you don't want to have to miss the encores, do you? There were several gigs we went to at the Odeon where we'd have to run out the building, run across Birmingham to catch the bus back to Stourbridge; otherwise we'd have been stranded in Brum. We walked back from Brum once, me, Sean and Dunc [Diamond Head's then singer and drummer Sean Harris and Duncan Scott], because we missed the last bus, and it took us about six hours!*

So it wasn't an easy ride for the album. the cover – a hand holding a giant razor blade, again courtesy of Roslav Szaybo – had supposedly led to some stores refusing to stock it because of the graphic image, although this was probably more the imagination of a dangerously overworked PR person than a story that had any basis in fact. In fact, Judas Priest's sixth studio LP was almost mired in controversy from the start. The original cover design had the blade cutting into the hand and spilling blood, although this was vetoed by the band. Then, in the weeks before the release of album in April 1980 – the time when maximising press interest is essential to get reviewers' attention and so guarantee column inches – it was revealed that *British Steel*'s master tapes had been stolen and were being held for ransom. Most of the music papers treated it as the scam it undoubtedly was – *Sounds* 'investigated the story at the time and could find no evidence to substantiate it' – and not only weren't the band particularly proud of what the publicists had come up with but they also found themselves endlessly apologising for it.

British Steel came to life at Startling Studios. In almost the same way as *Killing Machine* followed on from the 'Better By You, Better Than Me' session by using the same producer and the same studio, for the follow-up to *Unleashed In The East* the band hooked back up with producer Tom Allom and went back to familiar territory to repeat what appeared to be – and what certainly turned out to be – a winning formula.

In 1983 Phil Denton would be instrumental in the formation of NWOBHM act Elixir, but in 1980 he was 18 years old when he first heard the *British Steel* album. As a musician he's in no doubt how much it influenced him:

> *It changed my life. I'd started playing the guitar at 16 and, being a rock fan, was listening to various rock records and trying to learn from them. I already owned* Stained Class *and* Unleashed In The East, *but* British Steel *was the album that took Judas Priest to another level. And not only that, but I'd say that the* British Steel *album influenced a new generation of Eighties bands the same way as Black Sabbath's debut influenced the Seventies bands. The initial speed-picking intro of 'Rapid Fire' set the template for a faster-paced style of rock for a new generation.*
>
> British Steel *is full of great songs, one after another. 'Metal Gods', 'Breaking The Law' and 'Living After Midnight' are the obvious favourites that went on to become mainstays of the band's live set and so played their part in the band becoming megastars. But for me, songs such as 'You Don't Have To Be Old To Be Wise', 'Steeler' and 'Grinder' are just as important, both from a guitarist's point of view as much as a fan's. The thing about these songs are that they are fairly simple to learn as a budding guitar player but are still really strong songs in themselves. And just as importantly, they're fun! In the early days of Elixir, in between working on our own songs, we would often have a run-through of something like 'Breaking The Law' or 'Living After Midnight' just for our own enjoyment of playing them.* British Steel *is more than just a fantastic record: it's an inspirational album that led the way for rock and metal bands for years to come.*

'Rapid Fire' (Tipton / Halford / Downing)

One of the album's many joys is that opener 'Rapid Fire bookends it' and closer 'Steeler', two of the band's fastest, most exciting songs, riffed 'n' revved up with some great guitar work and choppy, semi-nonsensical but rhythmically interesting lyrics which bounce along like an LSD-filled Spacehopper. Downing even admits that 'there was no better track [to open the album] than 'Rapid Fire',' with its razor-sharp guitars, double kick-drum salvo and tongue-twisting middle eight, so why on earth the US arm of the record label opted to kick things off with the more genteel and radio friendly 'Breaking The Law' is anyone's guess. You can almost imagine the conversation in some exec's mahogany-panelled office: ''Rapid Fire'? You can't open a record with that; it doesn't even have a chorus,' and so the American version of *British Steel* is robbed of starting and finishing with two out-and-out rabble-rousers.

Another new drummer, another frenetic workout with which to introduce him – this is Holland's showcase and is a song with pace, stamina and fluid guitar breaks. It also introduces the verb 'to desolisate' to the English language.

'Metal Gods' (Tipton / Halford / Downing)

This mid-paced neckbreaker quickly became a fans' favourite and was promoted to an opening number in the Ripper Owens' years. Chosen as the flip to 'Breaking The Law' it's an easy ride for the whole band, really: no need to break into a sweat, but keep to the beat. In these days when you can buy a drum pattern off the internet, it probably sounds strange that effects in the Eighties were a little more mandraulic. You want to replicate the marching iron feet of the metal gods? Grab a tray of cutlery, and slam it down on a hard surface. Or the reaping of lives by the robots' scythes? Take a pool cue and swing it through the air. Simples...

'Breaking The Law' (Tipton / Halford / Downing)

Look up 'fun' in a dictionary and you'll find 'Breaking The Law', a song so well-known that in later years Halford didn't even have to sing it, but just turned the mic to face the audience and let them do the honours: its so-bad-that-it's-good video certainly helped the song achieve lifelong fame. 'Breaking The Law' is like a 'Ripper' for the Eighties, and despite the title, there's not an offensive note in its two-and-a-half minute running time, just florid riffing, some sirens and more cheap effects, this time achieved by dropping some milk bottles from a balcony to smash on the patio below. Ruddy hooligans!

'Breaking The Law' was the album's second single. Only available as a 7" and backed by 'Metal Gods' the record came in a wallet sleeve with a patch that was soon decorating many a denim jacket and waistcoat. Like its predecessor though it walked confidently up to the door of the Top Ten Club but failed to get past the bouncers, peaking at No.12, just like its predecessor.

'Grinder' (Tipton / Halford / Downing)

A bit of a B-side, this one – very straight, very ordinary – as it plods away for four minutes without ever really going anywhere, although in the live environment its hacking riff and Halford's vitriolic lyrics brought it to life. Not the best song on the album, it would appear as the B-side to 'United' where it should have been all along. It was one of Tipton's favourites though, as he mentioned to the *Sounds* duo of Geoff Barton and Ross Halfin. ''Metal Gods' is, to my mind, an all-time classic. It's got so much power. 'Grinder' is also one of my favourites. It's 150 per cent heavy metal.' Mind you, he also told them, '*British Steel* will become a new term for heavy metal, you mark my words.' Err, OK, Glenn, whatever you say...

'United' (Tipton / Halford / Downing)

A song with fewer friends than Mr Lonely's Facebook page, whatever the band might say 'United' was a blatant attempt to emulate the success of 'Take On the World' which failed miserably. The *Sounds* album review had called the track 'an unqualified dirge…', a point Barton and Halfin raised with Tipton. 'No, it's a great song,' Tipton offered in its defence. 'We don't really want to play 'Take On The World', but the kids demand it. I don't even like 'Take On The World' very much – 'United' is much better. If you listen to it, you'll realise it's really heavy metal. Wait until you hear us play it live, it's so heavy! Look, when you go home, listen to it again. I promise, after four or five plays you'll really like it.'

'Somehow, I doubt it…' the *Sounds* duo deadpanned.

Released to tie in with the band's Monsters Of Rock appearance it was the third and final single from *British Steel*, issued in a poster bag which, when opened, revealed the band on a studio frame. A live shot would have been more encouraging. It didn't actually flop – it reached No.26 which wasn't bad for two tracks taken from an album which had been out four months without a video to promote it. They did appear on *Top Of The Pops* again – on 28 August – lipsynching their way through one of their worst songs in front of a bunch of bopping and badly-dressed teenagers, but it is a truly terrible song which at three-and-a-half minutes is about three-and-a-half minutes too long.

'You Don't Have To Be Old To Be Wise' (Tipton / Halford / Downing)

'You Don't Have To Be Old To Be Wise' makes its libertarian viewpoint very clear and went on to become a stage favourite retired way too soon. Originally the opening cut of Side Two, the US release switched this with 'Living After Midnight'. Who knows why …

Skipping over *Point Of Entry* for a moment 'You Don't Have To Be Old To Be Wise' is an early ancestor of the likes of 'You've Got Another Thing Comin'. The message is in the title, the song is in no hurry to depart and overall the longest song on *British Steel* is an aural treat with a cracking split solo and ample scope for a live rendition singalong, although it dropped out of the set once the *Point Of Entry* tour was done and dusted.

'Living After Midnight' (Tipton / Halford / Downing)

Dum-dum dum-dum-dum … It all starts here, with a limited edition 12" single released on 21 March 1980. The story goes that Halford was trying to get some sleep in the early hours of the morning while, in the room below at Startling, Tipton was messing around with a riff he'd had in mind. The sleep-deprived singer appeared for breakfast with the lyrics which had come to him in bed. Hence, 'Living After Midnight', you see. Despite not being that good, with two live outtakes from *Unleashed In The East* on the B-side ('Delivering The Goods' and 'Evil Fantasies') and the price pegged at £1.15 it shot to No. 12 in the singles charts, earning the band their third *Top Of The Pops* slot in the process, and paved the way for *British Steel*'s runaway success. Unfortunately, as mentioned earlier, the night of the TV show's recording coincided with another show at the Birmingham Odeon and, running late, the band let their hometown crowd down for a second time.

'The Rage' (Tipton / Halford / Downing)

Metal/reggae crossover was all, well, the rage around that time. Scorpions had 'Is There Anybody There', Krokus 'Tokyo Nights' and Priest offered up this funky little beauty. 'The Rage' is a stunningly produced song, and well-crafted too: it's a shame the band never really trod this path again. Although you wouldn't have expected it to make the live cut it's certainly one of the album's highlights; it shows what the band were capable of when they thought outside the box.

'Steeler' (Tipton / Halford / Downing)

''Steeler' will become the headbanging song of the Eighties,' Tipton told Geoff Barton and Ross Halfin. 'When we did it in the studio K.K., and I got so carried away, our guitars were just like screaming feedback at the end.' So why did they play it on just the US dates and then discard it, you have to wonder. A crash 'n' burn to the run-off groove, 'Steeler' is the Priest classic that never was, being retired from the live set way too early. Again, the band throw away their own formulaic shackles to come up with a song with no chorus – not even a title line. After dispatching the verses, things are dominated by a playful guitar work-out over a pounding riff which begs to go on and on but which is cut off far too soon as Holland picks up the pace to wrap things up. At four-and-a-half minutes long, 'Steeler' is at least four-and-a-half minutes too short.

Post Album Events

The *British Steel* tour had kicked off on 7 March 1980 at Cardiff University and then ran through the UK until the beginning of April when the band moved on to Europe and then America. However, as the album hadn't been released in time for the tour the UK leg didn't actually feature any songs off *British Steel* at all, the band electing to continue with the *Unleashed In The East* set. But with 'Hell Bent For Leather' promoted to set opener one obvious omission from the set that trawled around the UK was opener 'Exciter', which gave rise to rumours that new drummer Dave Holland couldn't play it, another erroneous fact that Tipton was keen to put right in *Sounds*. 'Once and for all, I'd like to kill the rumour that he can't play 'Exciter'. Listen to 'Rapid Fire' on the album… It's much faster than 'Exciter', and Dave handles the drum parts really well. We'll be doing it on our next tour to prove it. [They didn't, by the way.] We only stopped playing 'Exciter' because we were sick of it.'

The support band for the tour were up-and-coming NWOBHM heroes Iron Maiden who did their job of warming up the crowd with aplomb, ratcheting up their fanbase at the same time and managing to upset their hosts with claims about blowing Priest offstage. The tour was extremely well received, and the reviewer from *Sounds* went overboard about the main attraction:

> *Having dropped 'Exciter' from the set (the rumour being that new drummer Dave Holland couldn't master the beat) Priest opened with 'Hell Bent For Leather', with Rob Halford being allowed, unlike the last time at Hammersmith, to ride his motorbike on to the stage. K.K. Downing and Glenn Tipton must be the best pair of heavy metal guitarists in existence. If you don't agree, try and name another duo that excites on stage like these two. Tipton handles most of the solos, and I think that it's fair to say that he is more of a soloist, while K.K. is more a riffer. But they both complement each other, unlike twin lead guitarists who tend to get in each other's way sometimes… When you consider that the tour was to promote the new album (*British Steel *– out at the end of the month), it was amazing that Priest didn't play any songs from it. But I suppose that when you've got a set of such high calibre, you don't need to chuck out any of the old favourites.*

The climax of the UK tour came at the Rainbow in London where, to celebrate 50 years of the Theatre, Levis' sponsored a series of shows, opening on Tuesday 1 April with Judas Priest and Iron Maiden. To mark this auspicious event – or maybe because his lycra stage wear was chafing – Halford decided to drop his tights and let it all hang out. In attendance that night, alongside Andrew Hanson, whose photo of the event appeared a couple of weeks later in *Sounds* with the vocalist's offending 'exciter' obscured by a black triangle, was Phil Denton. 'I do remember Halford dropping his strides at that gig – I think I remember a few people talking about it afterwards – although, like one of those football managers whose players commit some awful sin, I don't think I actually saw it; maybe I was looking the other way, headbanging, or a bit worse for wear from the beer. But it's not something that's etched in my memory, thank God!' he laughs. As the singer would later quip to Steve Gett, 'never was such a thing so big displayed to a crowd so small!' Well, it was April Fool's Day after all.

After two months' worth of touring the UK and Europe, in May Judas Priest found themselves back in America once more, where the earlier efforts to establish a foothold were beginning to bear fruit. One gig from the US leg of the tour appeared on CD in 1998 under the title *Concert Classics*. It's obviously not official – the rear tray photo is an outtake from the Les Binks-era backlit photo session used to promote 'Evening Star' and the front cover is another outtake, this time from the *Unleashed In The East* shoot – so how it came to see the light of day is a matter of conjecture, but as a souvenir of yet another tremendously exciting show that never reached the UK, it has few equals. Although there's no information on the release whatsoever, the show is from the Rainbow Music Hall in Denver on 25 June 1980; a later re-issue on The Store For Music label retitled it *Live In Concert 25 June 1980*, the cover aping *British Steel* with the hand holding not a razor blade but a Photoshop concert ticket.

With the US dates successfully completed, the band returned home where they had been invited to play at the first ever *Monsters Of Rock* festival at Castle Donington. At their previous UK outdoor festival appearance at *Reading* all those years ago, Judas Priest had been the second band to play; now they were second on the bill to Rainbow and followed Scorpions, April Wine, Saxon, Riot and Touch. Although as an outdoor event it took a while for Donington to find its feet this was the first true wholly metal festival in the UK and a real indication of Judas Priest's ever-growing stature. It would also be the last outdoor festival the band would play in the UK for thirty years, until they triumphantly headlined *High Voltage* in July 2011.

Things didn't kick off particularly well. As Allan Jones recounted in his hilarious, if somewhat discourteous and ill-mannered review in *Melody Maker*:

> *The night before there had been a full-scale dress rehearsal. Rainbow had intended to climax their show on Saturday night with the most violent explosion they could mount. They'd brought in cases of gelignite to do the trick. On Friday, at the end of their rehearsal, someone pulled the plunger, and the whole lot went off with a bang you might have heard in Nottingham. The stage survived the blast, but only just. Judas Priest's entire backline was blown out. Much of the PA suffered severe damage. One of the lighting rigs was severely buckled. The blast ripped through the tents and caravans behind the stage, throwing people from their seats, deafening those who had escaped cardiac arrests.*

But despite that upset things went pretty much to plan on the day and Judas Priest acquitted themselves admirably. *Sounds* despatched Geoff Barton and Robbi Millar to cover the event:

> *...I've no grumbles about Judas Priest. It's very true that they lay themselves wide open to more piss-taking than [Secret Affair frontman] Ian Page's mouth but I, for one, have become sooo bored with all the nudge-nudge presumptions regarding Rob Halford's sex life. Who cares if he fucks men, women or kangaroos? The suggestions make no difference to the music and Priest are still capable of knocking spots off 90% of the NWOBHM... Although something of a mess was made of 'You Don't Have To Be To Be Old To Be Wise', the album British Steel was well represented by 'Grinder' and 'The Ripper' was met by vast approval when it was*

> *pulled out from the past… Unfortunately, I don't know if either 'Breaking The Law' or 'United' were given an airing – I'm sorry about the former heartily grateful about the latter – on the whole, the band put on a wholly creditable show and it sometimes seemed a little demeaning that they were only second on the bill – especially judging by thousands of carefully sewn badges on display.*

Their set was a cut-down version of the US shows. After the appearance of Halford on his Harley and the bish-bash-bosh of the opening three songs – 'Hell Bent For Leather', 'The Ripper' and 'Running Wild' all being despatched in less than ten minutes – 'Living After Midnight' was one long singalong marathon which seems to have engaged a significant number of the assembled crowd. The first of three songs to be played from *British Steel* for the first time in the UK, the new-style hit single gave way to two of the band's elder statesmen 'Sinner' and 'Beyond The Realms Of Death'. The aforementioned 'You Don't Have To Be Old To Be Wise' and 'Grinder' brought proceedings back up-to-date before a storming version of 'Victim Of Changes' marked the end up the set with encores of 'The Green Manalishi (With The Two-Pronged Crown)' and 'Tyrant' wrapping up a triumphant sixty minutes. As well as being in top form vocally, Halford was also at his most playful, exhorting the crowd at one point to make 'as much noise as you like to tell those jets to fuck off!' as yet another plane flew overhead from East Midlands airport.

As a souvenir / money-making exercise, a live album from the festival *Monsters Of Rock* was rush-released by Polydor on 10 October, but unfortunately, Judas Priest were the only band unwilling and/or unable to contribute songs to it. The reasons for this have never really been fully explained, but it's a great shame as, for example, the version of 'Sinner' that Halford, Tipton, Downing, Hill and Holland blasted across Donington racetrack that day would have made a much better opener to the LP's second side than Rainbow's 'All Night Long' party piece.

With one final show, the *Neunkirchen Festival* in Nuremberg, the *British Steel* tour was, surprisingly, over. These days the album would have been toured for many, many months to come, but at what appeared to be the very height of their success with their most commercially successful album yet, the band were taken off the road and studio time was booked once again.

Almost forty years later I suggested to Downing that Judas Priest should have headlined Donington. I know it's all about scheduling and availability before you even start talking about money, but in the summer of 1982, or '83, or '84 or even '85 the band should have topped the bill at *Monsters Of Rock*. You could hear the disappointment in his voice when he simply replied: 'I know... Yeah, I know...'

Above & Below: The mighty Judas Priest – now featuring Richie Faulkner rather than founder member K.K. Downing on guitar – pictured at the High Voltage festival in London on 23 July 2011. At one point this was billed as the band's final ever festival appearance, which was then modified to their final ever outdoor festival appearance. History shows it was just another gig – but a cracker all the same!

Left: Where it (almost) all started for what would be now an almost unrecognisable Judas Priest – the test pressing for 'Holy Is The Man' and 'Mind Conception'.

Right: The artistic although seemingly irrelevant to the contents cover art of the *Rocka Rolla* LP. (*Gull Records*)

LEFT: *Rocka Rolla* 1984 Fame re-issue with the rather misleading and extremely metal *Steel Tsar* cover art (*EMI*)

Right: Forget *Rocka Rolla's* bottle top, this is much more like it! The striking cover art of Sad Wings Of Destiny, with its fallen angel, gothic script and first outing for the Devil's pitchfork design which would, much later, become almost a trademark for the band. (*Gull Records*)

Left: With *British Steel* taking the band to new heights, it was inevitable that Gull Records would see what they had in the vaults to capitalise on their former band's popularity. 1980 saw the release of this 12" single featuring 'The Ripper' [sic], 'Never Satisfied' and 'Victim Of Changes'. (*Gull Records*)

Right: Another such release was *Hero Hero* which came the following year and which pulled together most (but not all) of the band's two albums together with the Gull recording of 'Diamonds And Rust'. Great cover art, too. (*Gull Records*)

Left: The imposing cover art of *Sin After Sin* shot by Bob Carlos Clarke, who would go on to make his name as a cutting-edge fashion and glamour photographer. (*Sony*)

Below: Geoff Barton gets all worked up about *Sin After Sin* in his five-star review in *Sounds* in April 1977. Barton became one of the band's biggest champions, noting in this particular piece that 'Judas Priest have come of age...'

JUDAS PRIEST: split the Earth in two and let hellfire blaze.

Btoom! Pow! Blam! Whack! Slam! Crash!

(Or—Look out, Barton's gone bananas over the new Judas Priest album)

JUDAS PRIEST 'Sin After Sin' (CBS)*****

JUDAS PRIEST have come of age. Away from the stumbling block of Decca's so-called 'progressive' label, Gull records; away from their disastrous, Roger Bain produced debut album release 'Rocka Rolla'; away from even much-better-but-sadly-it-didn't-receive-the-attention-it-deserved second LP 'Sad Wings Of Destiny' . . . away from all the uncertain moments of the past and into the safe arms of CBS records and Roger Glover.

The result? A third cataclysmic platter 'Sin After Sin', an album that could stop an advancing Chieftan tank in its tracks and shake it apart into a pile of nuts 'n' bolts.

Brummie metal merchants Judas Priest have, with the LP, usurped Black Sabbath's throne with the minimum of bloodshed but with the maximum of volume. While the Sabs — sadly — now flounder in riff-churning, peace sign flashing monotony, Judas Priest fight to lace doom-laden, menacing heavy rock music with some fresh instrumental angles, some variation and, above all else, some *excitement*.

BTOOM! Just listen to the opening track, 'Sinner'. Souls in torment, damned for eternity, writhe in delicious lyrical agony as the twin guitars of K. K. Downing and Glenn Tipton riff interminably, splitting the Earth in two and letting hellfire blaze throughout the land.

BLAM! Along comes 'Starbreaker', steamrolling into town, handclaps, instruments grinding 'n' growling, ponderous, thunderous.

WHACK! 'Let Us Prey', a solemn holy atmosphere at once giving way to a maniacally speedy guitar riff, high pitched vocals, appropriate gasp-to-catch-a-breath pauses, great song construction-destruction.

POW! 'Diamonds And Rust', a mutation of the Joan Baez song, as perfect a headshaker as you're likely to find this side of 'Paranoid'.

SLAM! 'Call For The Priest/Raw Deal', weighty, leaden, cumbersome, metallic overload.

CRASH! 'Dissident Aggressor', rock 'n' roll Ragnarok, vocal speaker interchange, beginning on a thunderclap and ending on an instrumental atomic detonation.

Just great — and with the absence of a dispensably dorkish, overly romantic track 'The Last Rose Of Summer' and the deadly dull 'Here Come The Tears', 'Sin After Sin' would have been greater still.

And while singer Rob Halford goes over the top with the vocal gymnastics at times, and while Roger Glover's largely commendable production plays little attention to the subtleties of Judas Priest's music (for subtleties there *are*), 'Sin After Sin' remains the most powerful British heavy rock release for years.

What else can I say except — buy it? — **Geoff Barton.**

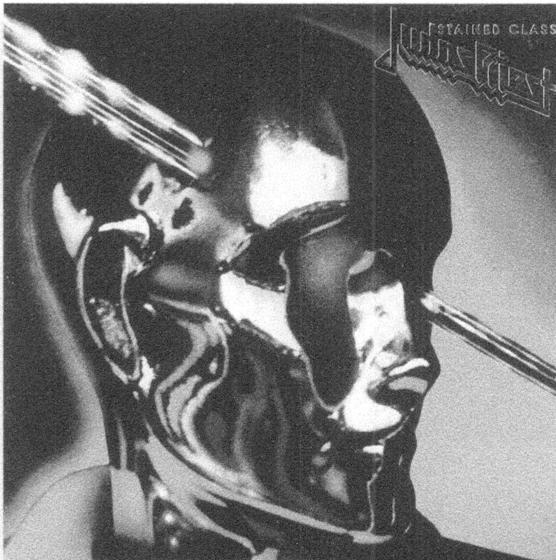

Left: 'Iconic' is a word that is often bandied about, but several Priest album covers are worthy of that status and 1978's *Stained Class* is one. The eye-catching design stood out in the racks and demanded attention. (*Sony*)

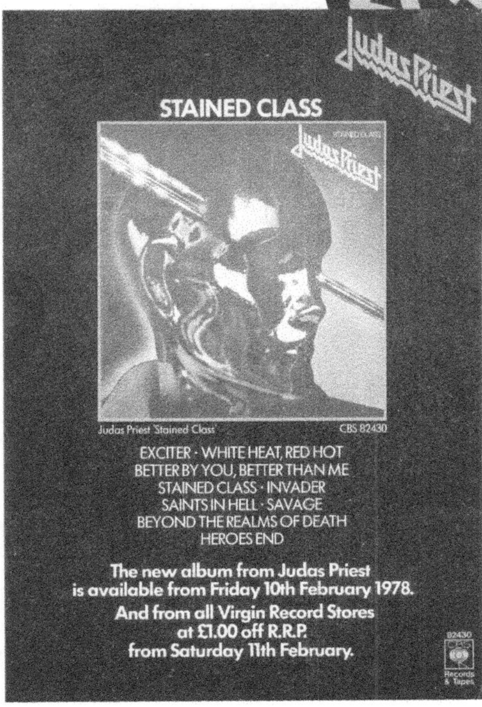

Above & Left: However, it looks like the LP sleeve blew the promotional budget, the four-side A4 1978 tour programme looking rather flimsy. The inside contained one page of text and one page of rather poor black and white photos, with an advert for *Stained Class* on the rear cover.

Left: Another iconic image, this time the UK *Killing Machine* cover. (*Sony*)

Right: 'Ma, I made it. Top Of The Pops!' to paraphrase Jimmy Cagney. The cover of 'Take On The World', the single that finally gave Judas Priest their long-deserved commercial breakthrough. (*Sony*)

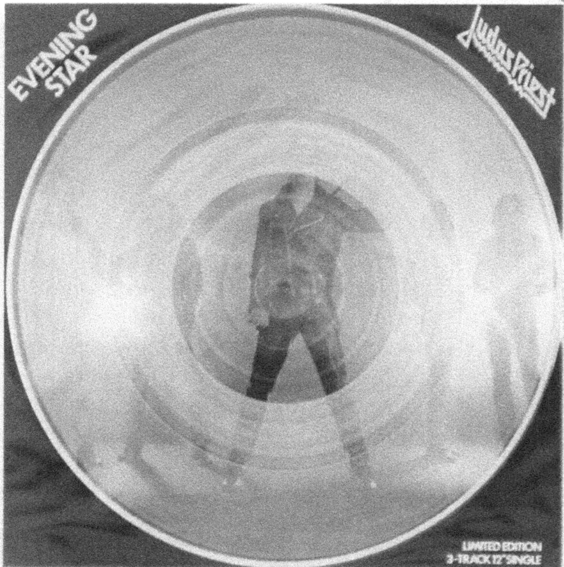

LEFT: A minor hit at the second attempt. The 12" clear vinyl re-issue of 'Evening Star' failed to hit the same giddy heights as 'Take On The World' but was a great package for fans to relish. (*Sony*)

Right: *Unleashed In The East* – still one of the Top Ten greatest live albums of all time, despite what detractors might think. Great album, terrible cover: the posed 'live' photos are all too obvious, as is the lack of drummer. There must have been one photo from the tour they could have used, surely...

It's cataclysmic . . .
It's blistering . . .
It's . . .

JUDAS PRIEST
'Unleashed In The East'
(CBS 83852)*****

BOW TO your knees and repent if you please, all of you who thought that Judas Priest had 'sold out' and had 'had it' just because they had the audacity to have a hit single, 'Take On The World'.

Yeah, get down on that floor and grovel, cringe and cower away from the cataclysmic live-recorded heavy rocking force of 'Unleashed In The East' . . . an album that is, quite simply, the *business*.

will, people being perversely attracted to them because of their – ahem – street credibility. No real slight meant on Nutz, after all I'm sure they'd like a hit single as much as anyone else (although admittedly a record deal would help), it's just the attitude that stinks.

Why can't the kids who wrote to *Sounds* slating Priest for crossing over to Peter Powell territory, abandoning their allegiance to them in the process, see that a chart-placed 45 is a *good thing*, it enables a group to make money and therefore put on shows, make better records and give everyone a better deal.

drink Tequila?!" – 'Unleashed In The East' plays the part of the boxer with the listener acting the punchbag. Fists flying, it's a case of wham bam, whop, bop till you drop, the vinyl equivalent of the pain/pleasure principle.

Of course we've already had live tasters in the forms of 'White Heat, Red Hot', 'Starbreaker' and 'Beyond The Realms Of Death' on the 'Take On The World' and 'Evening Star' 12 inch singles and even though bad production often robbed them of their full dynamics, they were nonetheless lip smacking starters for this long-playing main course.

It's blistering, breathless

Left: After the wholly undeserved drubbing handed to *Killing Machine* by *Sounds*' scribe Pete Silverton, it was good to have Barton back behind the typewriter to pen another five-star review for Priest's first live album.

Left: Iconic once again, the toned-down final version of *British Steel*'s artwork. The original version saw the blade biting into flesh with plenty of blood to upset people. (*Sony*)

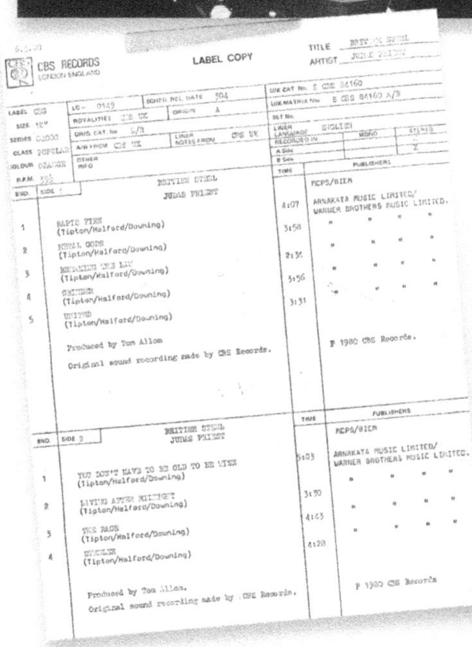
CBS RECORDS
LONDON ENGLAND
LABEL COPY
TITLE BRITISH STEEL
ARTIST JUDAS PRIEST

LABEL CBS
SIZE 12"
SERIES 00000
CLASS POPULAR
COLOUR ORANGE
R.P.M. 33⅓
LC- 0149
SCHED. REL. DATE 504
ROYALTIES CBS UK
ORIGIN A
ORIG. CAT. No. L/R
A/W FROM CBS UK
LINER NOTES FROM CBS UK
OTHER INFO
UK CAT No. S CBS 84160
UK MATRIX No. S CBS 84160 A/B
SET No.
LINER LANGUAGE ENGLISH
RECORDED IN
MONO
STEREO X
A Side
B Side

BND. SIDE 1
BRITISH STEEL
JUDAS PRIEST

BND.		TIME	PUBLISHERS
			MCPS/BIEM
1	RAPID FIRE (Tipton/Halford/Downing)	4:07	ARNAKATA MUSIC LIMITED/ WARNER BROTHERS MUSIC LIMITED.
2	METAL GODS (Tipton/Halford/Downing)	3:58	" " " "
3	BREAKING THE LAW (Tipton/Halford/Downing)	2:34	" " " "
4	GRINDER (Tipton/Halford/Downing)	3:56	" " " "
5	UNITED (Tipton/Halford/Downing)	3:31	" " " "

Produced by Tom Allom
Original sound recording made by CBS Records.
P 1980 CBS Records.

BND. SIDE 2
BRITISH STEEL
JUDAS PRIEST

BND.		TIME	PUBLISHERS
			MCPS/BIEM
1	YOU DON'T HAVE TO BE OLD TO BE WISE (Tipton/Halford/Downing)	5:03	ARNAKATA MUSIC LIMITED/ WARNER BROTHERS MUSIC LIMITED.
2	LIVING AFTER MIDNIGHT (Tipton/Halford/Downing)	3:30	" " " "
3	THE RAGE (Tipton/Halford/Downing)	4:43	" " " "
4	STEELER (Tipton/Halford/Downing)	4:28	" " " "

Produced by Tom Allom.
Original sound recording made by CBS Records.
P 1980 CBS Records

Left: A CBS sales sheet which accompanied the white label press and promo versions of *British Steel*. (*Sony*)

Right: The original Monsters Of Rock programme, with Judas Priest second on the bill to Rainbow. The best ever line-up at Castle Donington? You decide...

Right & Below: Another less-than-satisfying tour programme was the *British Steel* brochure. One of the first to feature virtually no text or tour dates, so it could be sold anywhere in the world, the A4 booklet featured a double-page spread for each band member and, in the centre pages, a pop-up Judas Priest stage set. Every home should have one.

Left: The not-at-all iconic cover of *Point Of Entry*. This and its US counterpart were described by K.K. Downing as 'the best ideas we had at that time.' (*Sony*)

Left & Above: The *Point Of Entry* tour programme again suffered from artists' block on the cover ("none blacker"!), although the German guest pass is a little more exciting.

Right & Below: Doug Johnson's epic artwork for *Screaming For Vengeance* (The Hellion) and *Defenders Of The Faith* (The Metallian), the two albums which broke the band in the States and finally assured their status as Metal Gods. (*Sony*)

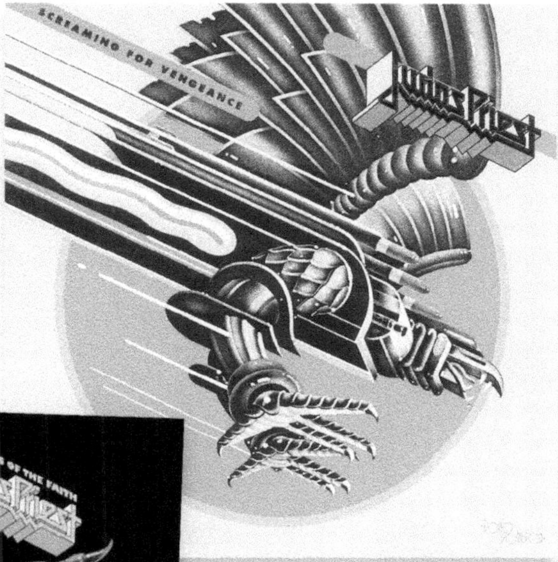

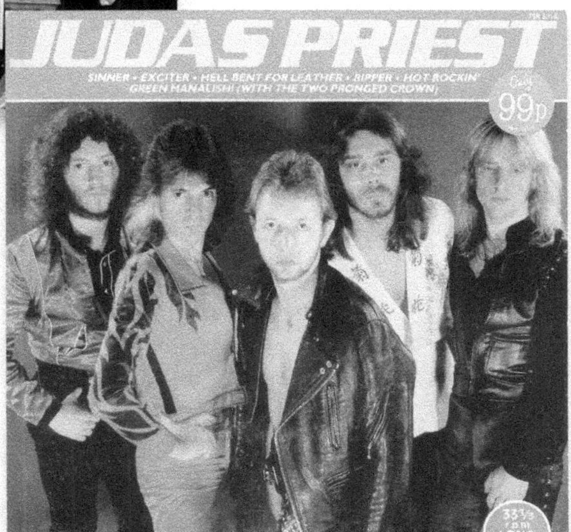

Right: Meanwhile, in the UK fans were treated to the rather curious *Scoop 33* six-track EP released in 1983. You have to assume that the band were not given the opportunity to approve the cover photo (another from this session had appeared in the *Stained Class* tour programme). *(Pickwick)*

Rob Halford ...

... K.K. Downing ...

... Glenn Tipton and Ian Hill, pictured at a US Festival in San Bernardino, California, on 29 May 1983

Right: The most divisive album in the band's catalogue. You can always start an argument by suggesting that *Turbo* is the band's best album. (*Sony*)

Left: Promotional flyer for the *Turbo* 30 re-issue, photographed by Mark Weiss. Note the lack of drummer - again. (*Sony*)

Right: Did no-one at the record company think this sleeve looked terrible? The front cover of *Priest... Live!* (*Sony*)

Left & Below: A change of artist brought in Mark Wilkinson for 1988's *Ram It Down* and the following album *Painkiller*, although by this time the writing was on the wall. (*Sony*)

LEFT: A rather eye-catching full-page advert of the 'A Touch Of Evil' single, listing all its multiple formats. (*Sony*)

Left: Fight's *War Of Words* album launch at Concrete Foundations Forum, September 1993. Drummer Scott Travis (towering over everybody else) jumped ship to sign up with Rob Halford's solo venture, but re-joined Priest in time for their 1997 *Jugulator* album. *(Lia Tucker)*

Below: Guitarists Glenn Tipton and K.K. Downing who, according to Downing's autobiography, never quite saw eye-to-eye. *(SPV)*

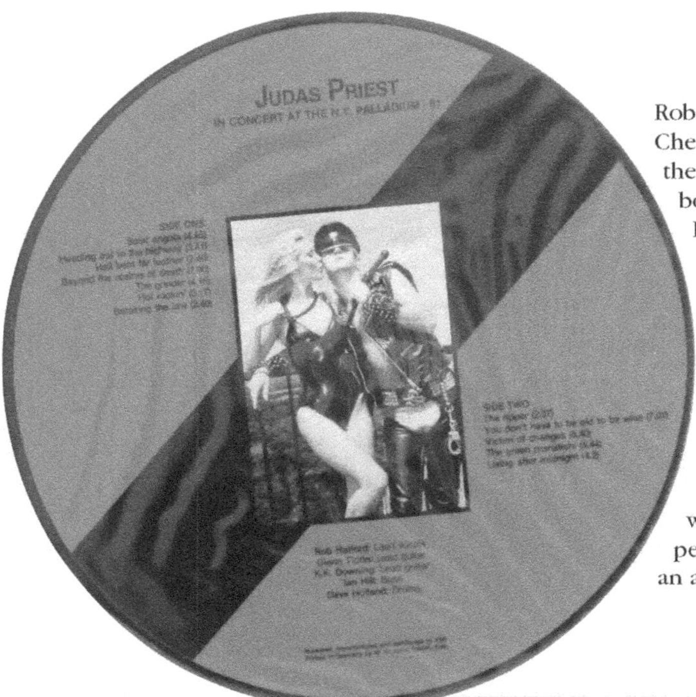

Rob Halford and model Cheryl Rixon, captured on the picture disc *Unchained* bootleg from the Palladium, New York, 1981, and again (from the same session) on the cover of *Live In Suisse*. Cheryl Rixon had already appeared with the band in the dodgy 'french maid' photospread in *Kerrang*! issue 10 which upset a lot of people but probably sold an awful lot of copies.

Point Of Entry (1981)

Personnel:
Rob Halford: lead vocals
Glenn Tipton: lead guitars
K.K. Downing: lead guitars
Ian Hill: bass
Dave Holland: drums
Record label: CBS
Recorded at: Ibiza Sound Studios, Spain, October-November 1980
Produced by: Tom Allom & Judas Priest
Release date: 26 February 1981
Highest chart positions: UK: 14, US: 39
Running time: 37:42

> *Point Of Entry is the best recording we've ever made* – K.K.Downing, *Sounds*

With Donington and the *British Steel* tour already in the past, Judas Priest regrouped at Ibiza Sound Studios, leaving behind the wet UK winter to bask in the sun. They were now tax exiles, and realising that as they were now starting to make – or at least aspiring to start to make – serious sums of money and having struggled for so long, the last thing they wanted to do was give it all to the tax man. The problem, however, was that Spain offered too many distractions in the shape of sunshine, sea, women and cheap booze, and wasn't really conducive to making a balls-to-the-wall follow-up to *British Steel*. So they didn't.

The result of their time in the Mediterranean, the first time they'd recorded an album outside the UK, was the disappointing *Point Of Entry*. The first real backward step in their career, *Point Of Entry* is an album with very little to redeem it in terms of critical appeal. It is what it is: appearing just ten months after *British Steel*, it's the sound of a band pulled off the road too early to bang out an album as quickly as possible while their star was still high in the sky, in case the success of *British Steel* had been no more than a flash in the pan. It was also very polished, very slick, just what US radio craved.

For their latest outing, the songwriters reverted to the ten-short-snappy-song formula of *Killing Machine*, with songs based largely on the verse-chorus-verse-chorus-solo-end approach, with just two tracks breaching the four-minute mark. It would have worked if the songs had been any good; unfortunately, they weren't. 'Heading Out To The Highway' and 'Desert Plains' are the only cuts of any note and bookend Side One, which also contained the two uneven singles and the throwaway 'Turning Circles'. Flipping the LP over just made matters worse: as the B-side to 'Don't Go' and upcoming tour opener 'Solar Angels' had a bit of bite, but the rest of the material is tiresome and completely uninspiring. It just doesn't sound finished; it sounds like a bunch of demos waiting for the real work to begin. And the band knew it, too; the only way they could think of describing it in the CD re-issue's booklet is as 'a brave album – the band have never been scared of trying to expand acceptable horizons of metal in this way.' They don't actually say that it's any good.

Once again the Americans couldn't resist monkeying around, this time with the sleeve. The UK version featured yet another cover by Roslav Szaybo, this time a hugely abstract design (unless I'm completely missing something) of land and sky separated by a sunset with a point (of entry) running from right-hand side to centre which might be a plane's wing tip or the snout of a very big penguin. It probably makes a very pleasing picture to hang in your front room, but it doesn't really scream out 'this is a heavy metal LP' like any of its CBS forerunners. The US and Japanese version carried a completely different cover, featuring a pathway, created from old-style computer paper, across a plain desert, with the title standing like a monolith at the point where path and horizon meet. Of the two sleeves, the UK release is less bad, but the alternative cover did introduce the '3D' version of the band's logo which would go on to be used up to *Turbo*. 'They might seem a little vague and unfocused to the casual observer,' is how Downing described the album sleeves in his autobiography, 'but they were the best ideas we had at that time.' One wonders what the outtakes looked like.

Point Of Entry is a wholly Marmite album though, and, writing in *Sounds*, Geoff Barton saw the album in an entirely positive light and awarded it a cracking four-and-a-half star review. He even claimed he only docked the final half-star because of 'the lack of a real bozo-metal anthem of the likes of 'Take On The World' or (especially) 'United',' although surely this must have been written with tongue firmly in cheek. But in his opinion:

> Point Of Entry *is perhaps the most devastating Judas Priest album to date… The Priest have been moving in a more basic direction since their* Killing Machine *LP, and this here is the payoff. While some may bemoan the passing of days of florid frenzy – as with the overblown 'Victim Of Changes' or the ridiculous 'Ripper' – I personally find this new JP music tremendously exciting … Less contrived and a deal more spontaneous than albums of old, track by track* Point Of Entry *grows into one massive metallic monolith… With drummer Dave Holland and bassist Ian Hill laying down simple steam hammer rhythms, with the dual axemen lurching in with licks as mindless as a lobotomised Halfin [an in-joke at the expense of* Sounds *photographer Ross Halfin] and with vocalist Halford growling with the ferocity of the tiger munching a missionary, Entry adds up to 40 minutes of champion chundering churnola.*

Soon-to-be Elixir guitarist Phil Denton was also impressed:

> *As the follow-up album to their masterpiece,* British Steel, *many young rock fans like me were waiting to see what Judas Priest would come up*

with next on their Point of Entry *record. Would it be as good as their previous album, now regarded as a classic? Or would they run out of steam? When I heard the album, I personally wasn't disappointed, although I think it's fair to say that it didn't quite reach the dizzy heights of* British Steel*. Songs such as the album opener 'Heading Out To The Highway', 'Hot Rockin'' and 'Desert Plains' are all very good; and 'Heading Out To The Highway' and 'Desert Plains' continued to feature in Priest's live shows for years to come.*

My personal favourites though, besides those three tracks, are the AC/DC-ish 'Troubleshooter' and 'Solar Angels' at the start of Side Two. I saw Priest on the Point Of Entry *tour at London's Hammersmith Odeon, and remember vividly the band opening the show spectacularly with the opening phased guitar of 'Solar Angels' playing as K.K. Downing and Glenn Tipton emerged up through the stage on hydraulic lifts. What an opening, and what a show! So whilst* Point of Entry *may not be held in such high regard from fans and critics as* British Steel, *it holds great memories for me, and it's an album I have a great deal of affection for.*

'When the record first came out I was a little bit disappointed because at first, I thought it wasn't really Judas Priest,' recalls Running Wild's Rock 'n' Rolf, 'but there were some songs on the album that I really liked from the first play like 'Heading Out To The Highway'; 'Hot Rockin'' was a really great track too. But the more I played the album, the more I discovered what a great record it really was. I really began to love all the songs on that album, and today it's a real classic in my opinion.'

Others weren't so impressed though. Satan's Russ Tippins sits in the naysayers camp and describes *Point Of Entry* as 'a very, well, innocuous album. I mean, after 'Desert Plains' and 'Heading Out To The Highway' and the other one – I'm struggling to think of any more tracks on the album; oh, 'Hot Rockin'', that's the one I was thinking of – it isn't very good, is it.' Hardly a glowing reference from a self-confessed fan of the band who, when his own band were between vocalists and had live dates in their diary, padded their set out with Priest covers.

Despite a promotional offer with *Sounds* that meant for the first few weeks you could buy the album for a special low price – the ploy being to guarantee early sales and a high point of entry in the album charts – it peaked at No.14 in the UK. Possibly even more disappointingly, it also peaked at No.39 in the US where it should have been more acceptable in terms of radio airplay than any of its predecessors. Neither UK single made the Top 50 either, 'Don't Go' stalling at No.51 and 'Hot Rockin'' at No.60. As for the videos, 'Don't Go' probably makes more sense after ten pints of lager and 'Hot Rockin'' is only really memorable for Rob Halford setting fire to his boots. As you do.

'Just because it's hot and sunny doesn't mean you can't come up with good heavy sounds,' Halford told Steve Gett, but the evidence didn't tally with the statement, and the fans who were served the album in February 1981 appeared to disagree. In the same book Tipton added:

> *I think what we were trying to achieve with* Point Of Entry *was to attempt something different and get a few things out of our system. In retrospect, I'd say it was a misunderstood LP. The music was very original and there were some classic tracks like 'Desert Plains', which I still enjoy listening to. I'll never regret doing it, even though the sales weren't as good as we might have been hoping for. But I'll always be quite proud of the record because it was a unique heavy metal album. We'll admit, though, it wasn't what people expected from us and I suppose it might have been a little self-indulgent.*

K.K. Downing confessed to Dave Ling years later that 'people don't understand how pressurised we were by the label, either to do covers or make hits. With that album, we gave them what they wanted.' Bad move. Please yourself, or please your fans, but don't go out of your way to please your label.

'Heading Out To The Highway' (Tipton / Halford / Downing)

If the album continued in the same way that it opened, *Point Of Entry* would be a different barrel of monkeys altogether. Featuring a mouth-watering dual solo from the guitarists, a catchy riff and some lyrical advice on getting out there and giving it your best shot 'Heading Out To The Highway' would go on to rightly take its place as a genuine classic. Although not a UK single it was released in The Netherlands, America and Canada as a 7" flipped with 'Rock Forever' and 'Hell Bent For Leather' from the *Unleashed In the East* recordings, but failed to interest the charts at all. Nice video though, in a cheesy kind of way.

'Don't Go' (Tipton / Halford / Downing)

As the album's first UK single, released as a taster in February 1981 and flipped with 'Solar Angels', 'Don't Go' was a bit of a let-down. It's dull and ploddy and never made the cut live, and although it's vaguely progressive at times it just doesn't do anything nor go anywhere, and three minutes and eighteen seconds later you have to wonder what the point of it was – if indeed there was a point at all. It peaked at a disappointing No.51 in the chart, and you would have thought that the record company would have realised by now that some previously unreleased live material on the B-side would have given a placing probably twenty places higher. The video shot for it wasn't really helpful, either; long-term collaborator and auteur Julien Temple must have been having an off day.

'Hot Rockin'' (Tipton / Halford / Downing)

The album's only really obvious single treads the same gaudy path as 'Living After Midnight' – 'the day is done, so let's get out there and get metalled'

– although sounds a lot more contrived than any of its predecessors in the singles market. The video clip, like the song itself, doesn't take itself too seriously, although isn't quite the rib-tickler that was 'Breaking The Law'. Despite CBS running it as a 7" in a picture sleeve coupled with a live version of 'Breaking The Law', and a 12" with a plain black sleeve but an exclusive centre label and an additional track live 'Living After Midnight' (both of the flipside songs are just credited as 'live February 1981' but are from the Amsterdam gig on 14 February) it stumbled at just No.60 in the UK charts, thus shooting down my earlier supposition about live B-sides guaranteeing chart success.

Promo singles are a whole different category in their own right, but a promotional copy of 'Hot Rockin'' with a completely different B-side, a really exciting live version of 'Steeler', was pressed up and sent to UK radio stations. Tommy Vance certainly gave the flip of his copy a spin on *The Friday Rock Show* (I've still got the cassette I taped off the radio here somewhere!) and the trade paper *Record Business* did list 'Hot Rock'' b/w 'Steeler' as the official release immediately prior to the actual official release hitting the shops. Why the change is anyone's guess but coupled with 'Steeler' live 'Hot Rockin'' would have been a much more attractive proposition.

'Turning Circles' (Tipton / Halford / Downing)

It's hard to know what's going on here. One of the many tracks that sounds like it never got past the demo stage – 'ah, that'll do; let's go to the pub' – and one which might have made a convincing single for the American market had it been given some TLC, 'Turning Circles' is a pop song with a heart of gold but feet of clay. The clipped intro makes for an interesting opening and is remarkably memorable too, but after that, it becomes a song of borderline interest and the Alan Partridge 'uh huh' vocal over an understated solo doesn't help as, unfettered, the guitar work might have rattled a few cages. Maybe it should have been handed to Toto. The band, not the dog.

'Desert Plains' (Tipton / Halford / Downing)

This is much more like it. The closing track of the album's first side would go on to become an enduring live favourite, at times enhanced by a drum break – isn't that what every song needs? – and an opportunity for Halford to show off his extensive vocal range. At its heart a love song, 'Desert Plains' is a bit of a chugger, but in a good way, and is also (at 4:37) the album's longest cut which perhaps shows what the band could have come up with if they hadn't been watching the clock when writing the material. Holland drives the track along with a driving beat which emulates the pulsing motorbike engine, and the solo is beautifully handled too.

'Solar Angels' (Tipton / Halford / Downing)

The opener on Side Two is quite an interesting number. A quasi-progressive cut with a solid, heavy riff but no chorus, 'Solar Angels' has a vibrancy akin to the lyrical magic of 'Dreamer Deceiver'. The opening chugging riff is an attention grabber in itself and made for an effective opening to the live shows when, as Phil Denton mentioned, the guitarists appeared through the stage floor on hydraulic risers. At a tad over four minutes, it's the album's second longest track, although it's only the two expertly delivered solos that extend it that far. It could have been more, really, but the band settled for less.

'You Say Yes' (Tipton / Halford / Downing)

From here it's downhill all the way to the run-off groove. Downing, Halford and Tipton could have got away with inserting one or two of the following songs to fill up a cracking album, but with the limited strength of the rest of *Point Of Entry,* the deficiencies of the album's last four songs are painfully apparent. Yes, they have their fans, but there's nothing approaching an even vaguely exciting song amongst them. 'You Say Yes' comes up first, and, although the cheated partner occurs a few times in the band's catalogue, aside from a razor-sharp riff cutting back in at around the two-and-a-half minute mark this is Priest at their worst and should have been consigned to the bin.

'All The Way' (Tipton / Halford / Downing)

An amalgamation of old back-catalogue ideas collide on this throwaway piece of power pop which, with a bit of work, would have fitted in much better later on *Turbo*. A spoken intro and handclaps add to the feeling of disaster as the song progresses, and indeed nothing can save it.

'Troubleshooter' (Tipton / Halford / Downing)

Well, it made the live set so the band must have thought it had some merits. A drum intro similar to 'Living After Midnight', a vocal delivery akin to 'Evil Fantasies', lyrics with no great merit… Bland and insipid, if it was a colour it would be beige. Once again you can only feel that we've been this way before, only better.

'On The Run' (Tipton / Halford / Downing)

The final track in this four-song chamber of horrors is a pseudo-AC/DC boogie stomp, the sort of song Angus Young and the boys used to record eight times to fill up any ten-track album. It's hard to believe that the band that had written and recorded 'Rapid Fire' and 'Steeler' earlier the same year would be reduced to peddling this fodder.

Post Album Events

'I suppose it [*Point Of Entry*] didn't have the correct ingredients for what you need to gain major recognition,' Halford later told Steve Gett, writing in *Kerrang!* 'To be quite honest I don't really know why it didn't do as well as I thought it would though – at the time I felt it was our strongest… Some people told me they reckoned the album was a bit self-indulgent and that we did things just for ourselves. I never viewed it that way, and we never approach albums like that.'

Nevertheless, the road beckoned, and the tour kicked off in February in The Netherlands (once again, before the album was in the shops) and saw the band playing across Europe until 8 March, when they wrapped things up at the Konserthuset in Stockholm. These opening dates saw a transition between albums, with five songs from *British Steel* ('Grinder', 'Breaking The Law', 'Metal Gods', 'You Don't Have To Be Old To Be Wise' and 'Living After Midnight') and just two – 'Troubleshooter' and 'Hot Rockin'' – from the upcoming release. With the band taking April off (presumably to munch their Easter Eggs) the US leg of the World Wide Blitz tour commenced on 4 May and kept the band on the road until the tail end of August. The early shows also saw the introduction of 'Solar Angels' as the opener together with 'Heading Out To The Highway' and 'Desert Plains'.

After another break, the band finally re-appeared in the UK, starting on 6 November in Hull and playing eighteen dates in all. 'Troubleshooter' had already been given the elbow (thankfully!), reducing the strike rate from *Point Of Entry* to four songs, but as a special bonus, the UK shows wrapped up with 'United'. How lucky are we! Another jaunt around Europe, this time with the emphasis more firmly on *Point Of Entry* than their previous dates, took them to their Christmas holidays and a much-deserved break.

Although much later a series of thirtieth-anniversary re-issues commenced with *British Steel* and continued through to *Turbo*, *Point Of Entry* was the one album from this run not to get a makeover. A shame, because although it will always remain the runt of the litter (controversial, possibly, but *Rocka Rolla* is arguably a more cohesive, more truthful and, well, better album than *Point Of Entry*) its tour featured two cracking radio broadcasts and subsequent bootlegs, one from The Palladium, New York, on 23 July, and the second recorded by the BBC at Hammersmith Odeon on 21 November. Adding both of those to a re-issue of *Point Of Entry* would have turned an ailing single CD into a must-have triple set.

Back in January 1982 though, the band were bizarrely despatched back to Ibiza Sound Studios for their next album which, realistically, had to be a killer.

Screaming For Vengeance (1982)

Personnel:
Rob Halford: lead vocals
Glenn Tipton: lead guitars
K.K. Downing: lead guitars
Ian Hill: bass guitar
Dave Holland: drums
Record label: CBS
Recorded at: Ibiza Sound Studios, Spain, January – May 1982 [also Bayshore Studios, Coconut Grove, Florida, credited on the LP only for the mixing]
Produced by: Tom Allom
Release date: 17 July 1982
Highest chart positions: UK: 11, US: 17
Running time: 38:42

> Screaming For Vengeance *is not only Judas Priest's best LP, but one of the finest to emerge this century… I've never been more excited by a hard rock album since the day I put the first Van Halen effort on the old turntable* – Steve Gett, *Kerrang!*

Despite *Point Of Entry*'s shortcomings, band and label chose to stick with the same formula for the next album but came out with a very different result. Cometh the hour, cometh the band…

After the relative disappointment of their previous album Judas Priest needed a substantially new game plan, and the one they came up with was simply entitled *Screaming For Vengeance*. This was the album they simply had to make and, together with its sibling *Defenders Of The Faith*, *Screaming For Vengeance* catapulted Judas Priest into the forefront of traditional metal. Whether by luck or by design – and it doesn't matter which – they delivered the goods in the finest style available, and July 1982 saw Rob Halford, Glenn Tipton, K.K. Downing, Ian Hill and Dave Holland (yes, three albums in and he's still there, now holding the record for consecutive studio album appearances!) deliver their metal masterpiece. *Screaming For Vengeance* has sold in excess of five million copies and was certified as a double platinum seller in America and platinum in Canada as well.

Rather oddly, there was no advance single to trumpet the album's approach, although *Screaming For Vengeance* isn't really a singles-orientated album, hence the employment of an outsider in Bob Halligan Jnr to come up with something more radio friendly. Two singles would follow, but neither set the world on fire. The album did come with a free poster though, a splendid 24" x 24" enlargement of the striking album cover, as well as an inner sleeve with lyrics and a magnificent mean 'n' moody black and white portrait of the band. The album's price was pegged at £3.99 for quite some time in the UK where despite all these 'extras' it disappointingly foundered just outside the Top 10.

Across the Atlantic, though, it was a different story altogether, as it gave the band their best ever US chart placing. As a result of this, or possibly because of this, the World Vengeance tour kicked off in Bethlehem, Pennsylvania, on 26 August 1982 and finally wrapped up at the US Festival in San Bernardino, California almost a year later on 29 May 1983, with the band needing just one trip to the Bureau De Change to exchange some US dollars for their Canadian counterparts. They would finally appear back in the UK for a string of eight dates in December 1983 (broken by a quick trip to Germany for the Rock Pop festival in Dortmund), ostensibly to promote their next album. But as with *British Steel*, this was yet to be released, which seemed to make the whole exercise a bit, well, futile (although hearing the *Screaming For Vengeance* material in the UK, at last, was, of course, very welcome). Downing would later note in his autobiography:

> *If I'm really being honest, maybe there was part of me that was thinking, US audiences have been much kinder to us than British ever have been. Let's focus on delivering the goods there. Was that a mistake? In retrospect, it probably was … But you can't take these decisions back. You can only do what you think is best for the band at the time. And to us,* Screaming For Vengeance*'s success in the States vindicated us, as have its cumulative sales. I guess we all thought, we'll get back to the UK before too long…*

Sounds' Philip Bell gave the album a very respectable four stars in a rather rambling review which took as its basic tenet the fact that the Seventies were over and that the band had drawn a line under their previous releases. However, he felt later albums hadn't been that fulfilling – 'after a few spins of *British Steel* or *Point Of Entry* as a matter of religious ritual you cast aside these chapters as stiff, simple run-of-the-mill sermons.' But the future, as Bell saw it, was bright:

> *…It's time to accept that the 'Island Of Domination' is deserted, that 'Stained Class' is fading and 'Exciter', 'Dissident Aggressor', the 'Saints In Hell' et al. are dead and gone. The latest possible epitaph was the titanic live album which was, I suppose, a perfect bridge, updating classics to contemporary Eighties' mightiness. Updating them, that is, to an age where Judas Priest is synonymous with all that is heavy metal… But there is life beyond the realms of death! Because* Screaming *marks the viperous vicar's return with all the Vengeance threatened in the title, with a communion of ye olden songs' intricacy – though not subtlety – and the Pagan thunder tilt towards today's trend for All Out Metal… So forget the Sinner. Long live the Hellion!*

'The Hellion' (Tipton / Halford / Downing)

The album's artwork features an apocalyptic robotic bird, the Hellion, the first of three consecutive covers by Doug Johnson, and although the rear sleeve carried a short backstory about this 'winged warrior' the song of the same name is a short instrumental which screams 'intro tape' and which, of course, was precisely that on numerous tours. Beautifully constructed, (and commercial enough to be the soundtrack to a Honda Odyssey advert) it crackles with excitement and is the perfect gateway to the album, giving way as it does to…

'Electric Eye' (Tipton / Halford / Downing)

A finer song about a spy satellite you will never find! A combination of the Orwellian nightmare, the misuse of technology and Cold War paranoia come together in this three-and-a-half minute workout about totalitarianism and the surveillance state which pretty much showcases everything Judas Priest have to offer in one bite-sized chunk. It's frenetic, it's well-structured, Halford uses his voice to great effect, the guitar work is exemplary, and there's a cracking solo by Tipton. Lyrically it's interesting too, updating the sci-fi theme into present-day actuality – had it been written for *Stained Class* it would have been considered fantasy, but by 1982 this concept was tempered with reality.

A live favourite, and the perfect way to get things into gear, 'The Hellion' and 'Electric Eye' coupling would open the tour, and be resurrected as the opener on the *Ram It Down* trek and then the comeback Angel Of Retribution tour in 2005. The pairing literally screams 'Judas Priest'. What more do you need?

'Riding On The Wind' (Tipton / Halford / Downing)

The album – and the live show – continues with another belter, just to show that the opening four or so minutes weren't a fluke. After a fairly easy ride with the opening cuts Holland gets to show he's still got the muscle when it's needed, and it's his drum fusillade that brings matters to order. More helium-pitched vocals from Halford, another great solo workout and an attention-grabbing finale, all packed into a track that's done 'n' dusted in a tad over three minutes, come together to prove that, sometimes, less is indeed more. It's not a song whose lyric demands a great deal of examination, especially after Tipton's quote in *Sounds*: 'We do ride the wind quite a bit, especially after too much lager the night before.'

'Bloodstone' (Tipton / Halford / Downing)

Inevitably, things would have to decrease in tempo somewhat, and 'Bloodstone' is the perfect way to bring things down to earth, in more ways than one. In an interview with Philip Bell Halford revealed that 'Bloodstone' was a term he used 'to describe the Earth. It's probably best described as a heavy metal peace song' which is there, obliquely, in the words he sings. It's a charming, mid-paced piece of music, although nothing really to get excited about, despite Holland thumping seven bells out of his kit. *Screaming For Vengeance* was massively plundered for the live set (at the second show of the tour, in East Troy, Wisconsin, eight of the album's ten songs are recorded as putting in an appearance) so it's no surprise that 'Bloodstone' made the cut.

However, it was soon put to bed when material from *Defenders Of The Faith* was ready to roll.

'(Take These) Chains' (R. Halligan Jr)

No-one really seems to recall who drafted in Bob Halligan Jnr's song to add an obvious single to the collection of material, although the band had never been averse to working with material written by others. This time – as with many other songs written outside the camp – it didn't really work for Priest, although it did Halligan's career no end of good. It lead to collaborations with the likes of KISS, Kix, Joan Jett, Helix, Blue Öyster Cult, Cher and many others, and furthered his own musical career with his band Ciele Rain.

The second single to be drawn from the album, the track was released in October 1982 under the shortened title of 'Chains' on the sleeve, although the centre label carried the full song title. After the surprise mini-success of 'You've Got Another Thing Comin'' it unexpectedly failed to chart at all, which must have surprised those who'd wanted the song recorded purely to give the album some commercial clout. The review in *Sounds* lampooned the single – 'now this is more what you're after – muscular, masculine machismo with an oh so obvious double entendre – It's all about how us soppy emotional women tie you down.' But it was written by someone – sorry, I don't have the name – who in another review on the same page wrote: 'I must confess I loathe heavy metal.'

The strange thing about the record is that if CBS wanted a hit single so badly, why didn't they invest in a video clip for it? Even more odd is the B-side. Eschewing the usual album track or live cut or previous material or throwaway outtake or whatever that often lurks on the back of a single someone came up with the idea of 'The Judas Priest Audio File – A Musical Biography' (or, as the adverts had it, 'eight minutes of riffs, rabbit and rock'), in which an unnamed narrator – Tom Allom? – talks through the rapid-fire history of the band interspersed with short snippets of 'Sinner', 'Exciter', 'Beyond The Realms Of Death', 'Take On The World', 'Breaking The Law', 'United', 'Living After Midnight', 'Solar Angels', 'Hot Rocking', 'The Hellion', 'Electric Eye', 'Take These Chains', and 'You've Got Another Thing Comin''. The script is pretty terrible, and the description of *Point Of Entry* as 'a point if not a milestone in their career' is particularly unhelpful, being as it can be taken in two completely different ways. As a B-side it's an interesting curio, but not the sort of things that would entice fans to part with hard-earned cash and '(Take These) Chains' went the same way as many a Priest single – straight into the bargain bins.

Trivia fans might like to note that the B-side of this 7" single played at 33 rpm while the A-side span at the more usual 45 rpm.

'Pain And Pleasure' (Tipton / Halford / Downing)

In any treasure chest, some things are going to be more valuable than others, and although 'Pain And Pleasure' isn't a bad song, set amongst these other glowing gems like '(Take These) Chains' before it it's more a silver bauble than a golden bangle. It's an unashamed, unabashed sadomasochistic number, whether you take it literally in the BDSM kind of way or in terms of an abusive relationship. It's a change of tempo, and at four-and-a-quarter minutes it's the longest song on the album so far, but it's a bit of a plodder and not something that you'd expect to hear in concert and this and '(Take These) Chains' are the two songs from that album that never made it into the live arena. Like a good thrashing, it has its fans, but I've never been convinced that the lyrics actually fit with the song's mood and, despite a really interesting solo, 'Pain And Pleasure' doesn't really close the album's first side with any great degree of satisfaction.

'Screaming For Vengeance' (Tipton / Halford / Downing)

After six shorter, snappy songs Side Two of the old LP offered up four longer, more intricate pieces of work, starting with the album's title track and *tour de force*. With one of the most explosive intros ever written 'Screaming For Vengeance' is the album's attention-grabber, cut from a similar cloth as 'Exciter' and 'Rapid Fire'. Given that 'The Hellion' / 'Electric Eye' had to open the record, the only place this song could go was at the start of Side Two, and like its forerunners 'Screaming For Vengeance' has everything required of a Judas Priest classic – frenzied vocals, powerhouse drums, a rock-steady bass line and some of the most exquisite guitar work put to tape. If this song doesn't get you going then you'd better check you're not on a mortuary slab.

In a similar way to 'Savage' it takes the side of the oppressed against the oppressor, although can be taken at anything from a global to a one-on-one situation. It's very clever lyrically, and also musically too. In terms of recording, Allom would tell Rock Candy magazine that 'Screaming For Vengeance' itself wasn't very easy. It was quite fast, and to this day I still can't work out the timing on the intro. I don't think anyone can! It was quite difficult to mix and also pretty hard for Rob to sing, purely because there were an awful lot of words in the song so cramming them in was tricky.'

'You've Got Another Thing Comin'' (Tipton / Halford / Downing)

One of the most enduring songs from the album, 'You've Got Another Thing Comin'' almost didn't make the cut. It wasn't until the final mixing took place in Florida that the band realised that they had the makings of a hit of their hands – the ultimate feelgood driving song. But, more prosaically, the album was coming in a bit short, and 'You've Got Another Thing Comin'' was cobbled together from some odd ideas to make up the running time. Just like 'Paranoid'. And just like Sabbath's calling card, *Screaming For Vengeance*'s final filler track became one of their most famous songs.

Allom recalled it differently to Xavier Russell, saying that the album was recorded in two chunks, as 'the band's management decided to stop the recording process for a four-month hiatus. So what ended up happening was that we laid down five or six songs in Ibiza over a couple of months, then recorded the rest of the songs in a studio in Florida [Bayshore] where we also mixed the album.'

'You've Got Another Thing Comin'' is another of those songs that split the fanbase, as some like its sweeping simplicity, but for others, it just chugs away interminably, eking out every one of its 305 seconds in a painfully repetitive manner. Nevertheless, US radio took to it like a duck to water and Downing admits that 'it was everywhere; every time you turned on the radio it seemed to be on ... There's no doubt that it was the song that broke us in America.' The single was issued as a regular 7" and a picture disc as well, with 'Exciter' from *Unleashed In The East* unimaginatively lurking on the flip; the US version coupled it with 'Diamonds And Rust'. And although it wasn't a massive chart success (No.66 on this side of the Atlantic and No.67 in the States) it was the icing on the cake in terms of the band's popularity in America and would book its place in Priest's live set, becoming an ever longer singalong piece, which really must have annoyed those that didn't like it in the first place. Time for a quick trip to the bar, anyone?

The opening line to this song about living for the moment was cleverly reprised as the finale to *Turbo*'s 'Parental Guidance' a few years later. In fact, some might argue that's the best thing about the whole song. And, incidentally, if, like me, you tend to be a bit of a stickler about grammar, then the original phrase for someone who's gravely mistaken was actually 'you've got another think coming'. *The Guardian Online* even ran a piece on this, putting the blame tongue-in-cheek on Priest's song for the popularity of the grammatically incorrect but now universally accepted 'another thing coming'. Just an observation!

'Fever' (Tipton / Halford / Downing)

This is the eighth song to make the live cut, the one that has the dubious distinction of being played once or twice on the *World Vengeance Tour* before being dropped. Halford would admit to it being 'a love song, I suppose. What I'm trying to do with Priest's lyrics on this album is make the music more accessible again to more and more people.' It's the album's longest song and Tipton would claim it to be 'one of the best things I've ever done.'

It is an intricate piece, a bit of a wolf in sheep's clothing, and although you can hear why it's probably not a great one for the stage, it's definitely one for the headphones. There's a lot going on within the structure, and when it gives way to the almost valedictory section around the 3:30 mark, the song simply soars. Not one to make it onto Best Of compilations, it's another overlooked classic, and it might have been more revered had it closed the album, instead of...

'Devil's Child' (Tipton / Halford / Downing)

I could upset people here, but this to me is the album's so-so song, which is why it's been slipped in right at the end. It's not as throwaway as the last few cuts on *Point Of Entry* and there's more to it than 'we've done three minutes, let's hit the bar,' but the backing vocals are Mickey Mouse, the lyrics – again about abuse of power within a relationship – aren't that great (another great rhyme occurs in 'your condition breeds ammunition') and like a marshmallow, it's wholly insubstantial.

Post Album Events

As mentioned earlier, Judas Priest spent all their tour support budget on a lengthy trek around the States, with a few dates in Canada. The *World Vengeance Tour* actually finished in Honolulu on 20 February 1983 but with the one further date at the US Festival in San Bernardino, California – the DVD of which accompanied the thirtieth anniversary release of the album – three months later Tipton and Downing decided it wasn't worth coming home (to either the UK, or to Spain where they now also had properties) so passed the time playing golf in Hawaii. As you do.

The US Festival was a massive event – the official attendance was 300,000 people – with the second day being given over to metal, and luminaries drawn from the likes of Quiet Riot, Mötley Crüe, Scorpions and headliners Van Halen trod the boards. The band were taken by helicopter to the site, a moment which Downing admitted made him feel 'that we really have made it to the top table – and that there was no going back.' 'Another excellent set,' reckoned *Kerrang!*'s Laura Canyon of Priest's appearance, sandwiched between Ozzy Osbourne and Triumph, 'well-paced, well-posed and well-lit, though lacking the elaborate Meccano set stage props of their last tour. There's 'Green Manalishi', great festival stuff, 'Screaming For Vengeance', a nice 'Another Thing Coming', with an instrumental bit for us all to sing and clap along with, and the bike too for the encore 'Hell Bent For Leather'.' The DVD captures the event in all its splendour, but it's obvious from the CD's booklet that pictures of the band onstage have been carefully chosen to airbrush drummer Dave Holland out of the equation, following his arrest in 2003 and conviction for sexual abuse the following year. Tellingly, in the one shot in which he features the rest of the band are in colour, but his image fades to black and white. Protesting his innocence to the end, Holland died in Spain on 16 January 2018.

Meanwhile, though, back in 1983, with the massive festival date under the belts, the sound of 300,000 fans ringing in their ears, and new management in the form of Bill Curbishley, the band flew straight back to Ibiza again to repeat the formula once more. Although this time they found that things weren't quite as they left them.

Defenders Of The Faith (1984)

Personnel:
Rob Halford: lead vocals
Glenn Tipton: lead guitars
K.K. Downing: lead guitars
Ian Hill: bass guitar
Dave Holland: drums
Record label: CBS
Recorded at: Ibiza Sound Studios, Spain, May-August 1983 (the original album just states that the album was recorded 'in Europe')
Produced by: Tom Allom
Release date: 4 January 1984
Highest chart positions: UK: 19, US: 18
Running time: 39:43

> *I think a lot of people are going to be very, very impressed with this record. The success of that last album meant a great deal to us. It gave us the boost to want to go in there and match the success of* Screaming For Vengeance *and also try and set things up for 1984 because, as far as production and every else goes on this album, it probably has the most impact and is the most interesting HM LP I've heard in a very, very long time* – Rob Halford, *Kerrang!*

If something's worth doing well, it's worth doing twice, and immediately after the US Festival, Judas Priest were back in Ibiza Sound Studios to create what is pretty much the baby brother of *Screaming For Vengeance.* This included the album being the same number of tracks (except instead of an intro this time around there was an outro) and the same outside songwriter to give the album some commercial spin, which, again, didn't really work. *Defenders Of The Faith* didn't come with a free poster, although there was an insert with which you could win one of three Suzuki motorbikes with six prizes of tour jackets for the runners-up. An inner sleeve carried the lyrics and live photos of the band (this time in full colour though, whereas for *Screaming For Vengeance* the inner sleeve was strictly monochrome). The cover was again by Doug Johnson and featured another beast, the Metallian, a futuristic tank with the head of a lion (metal lion, geddit?) and as a nod to the past, the spelling of said beast's name on the rear sleeve turned the 'T' into the Devil's Pitchfork insignia that had graced the neck of the fallen angel on *Sad Wings Of Destiny*. The Metallian would form the basis for the impressive stage set, as captured on the 'Love Bites' video clip. Tipton even admitted to *Sounds'* Steve Gett that the album had 'all the basic elements of *Screaming For Vengeance* and it runs along the same basic formula. That wasn't intentional – we didn't set out to come up with an exact copy. That's just the way we write these days.'

The result? Sit ten Priest fans in a room and five will say that *Defenders Of The Faith* is the better album and five will argue for its predecessor, but the one pertinent fact is that, for the first time in their career, the band had released an album which charted higher in the US than in the UK. If it is indeed true that wherever you lay your hat is your home, than the band's collective headgear lay on American beds.

Recreating the magic that was *Screaming For Vengeance* didn't come easy at first though. What Rob Halford, K.K. Downing, Glenn Tipton, Ian Hill, Dave Holland – yes, he's still there! – and Tom Allom didn't know, when they stepped off their plane at the end of May, was that Ibiza Sound Studios now only existed in name only. Hard times had meant that the gear, right down to the final microphone and coffee-stained mug, had been repossessed by the bailiffs. The owner had been waiting on an advance of Priest's fees, but if this could be sent early, the equipment could be released from hock and recording could commence. Accordingly, the money was transferred, and for a few days, the band lazed on the beach and worked on their tans until they had a call to say that the owner now had the desk back, although this was perhaps a little economical with the truth.

The recording desk had been unloaded on the roadside, at the foot of the hill which led to the studio. One thing even the staunchest critic would have to admit about Judas Priest is that the band had never been prima donnas, and instead of pulling the 'rock star' line they managed to roll the desk – with the aid of some logs – up into the studio, and then re-assembled the rest of the kit. Downing reckoned it took about four days to get everything into shape, and then, finally, the tapes were ready to roll. The band worked through the summer, and then the album was mixed in Florida from September to November, finally appearing in the shops as the New Year's hangovers were dissipating.

In the meantime, with nothing else happening in terms of releases, in the UK budget label, Pickwick released a rather curious six-track 7" EP in their Scoop 33 series which played at 33rpm (the clue's in the title) and cost just 99p. The rather bizarre mix of tracks ('Hell Bent For Leather', 'Ripper', 'Exciter', 'Hot Rockin'', 'Sinner' and 'Green Manalishi (With The Two-Pronged Crown)' – somehow they'd lost the definite article), low price and ridiculous cover photo in which none of (the Les Binks era of) the band look particularly good made it relatively collectable, and filled a gap in the collection while waiting for a new release to appear in the shops. 'Ripper', 'Exciter', and 'The Green Manalishi…' were straight off *Unleashed In The East*, incidentally, while 'Hell Bent For Leather' was the album cut, 'Hot Rockin'' the 7" edit and 'Sinner' was a heavily abridged – emasculated, in fact – version of the *Sin After Sin* track. It's perhaps worth noting that CBS had also released earlier in the year a cassette EP in their Original Greatest Hits series which consisted of 'Breaking The Law', 'Living After Midnight', 'Take On The World' and 'United'. Obviously, neither really clocked up any great number of sales.

Judas Priest returned to the UK in December 1983, pretty much two years since their last dates in their homeland. Once again they were treading the boards before the album had been released so the dates, which started on 12 December at Newcastle City Hall and finished ten nights later with the second of two shows at Birmingham Odeon, featured a hybrid set with 'The Hellion' / 'Electric Eye', 'Riding On The Wind', 'Bloodstone', 'You've Got Another Thing Comin'' and the title track from *Screaming For Vengeance*. Also included were a collection of old favourites and 'Freewheel Burning' as the sole representative of the new LP (which should already have been released as a single but for whatever reason this hadn't happened). In the midst of the run of nine dates, the band raced off to Dortmund for the Rock, Pop, Heavy Metal Festival on 18 December where the *Kerrang!* reviewer noted 'they were a spectacle to behold.' *Kerrang!* also covered the Hammersmith Odeon show, writer Mick Wall rambling on a little but noting:

> *What can I say about Judas Priest that will prove illuminating after all these years? I mean, everyone knows the band are premier deluxe models, built to thrill ... You don't review Judas Priest, don't be asking me to do that, you just get into it or do the other thing. Friday night's show was one you would have wanted to get into, I have never seen them perform better.*

'Freewheel Burning' (Tipton / Halford / Downing)

The album's opening cut was also issued as its first single, and although you wouldn't think it was chart-worthy 'Freewheel Burning' did hit No.42 in the UK on its release in January, buoyed by yet another vaguely ridiculous promo video clip. The 7" single was backed by 'Breaking The Law' while the 12" added 'Another Thing Comin'' [sic], both taken from the US Festival the previous May. At the time, in a number of interviews, the band stressed that they'd mixed 'Freewheel Burning' and sent it for release prior to the UK dates. However, the record company had held back until they'd heard the full album in case there was a better single, which meant that it was completely unknown by the UK crowds at those December dates. Ah well, at least they can say that they heard it first.

What's interesting about the 12" version is that it features a short intro from Downing and Tipton before the guitars really kick in which adds to the running time (this version clocks in at 5:02 whereas the album track is listed at 4:23) and which has never been made available on CD. The *Kerrang!* review noted that 'Freewheel Burning' is 'a 90mph gallop around every HM cliché ever written and thoroughly brilliant.' That's a pretty good synopsis, although it's worth adding that Tipton's solo is a real finger-twister and that if ever a song lived up to the quote attributed to Samuel Goldwyn about beginning with an earthquake and building up to a climax, it's this one. It's little wonder that the song's working title was indeed 'Fast And Furious'!

'Jawbreaker' (Tipton / Halford / Downing)

Maintaining the tempo, 'Jawbreaker' opens with a five-punch onslaught before Halford opens up over a simple dual guitar riff and then everyone else races to catch up. It's another example of Priest keeping their pedal to the metal, and although it's not the best song in their canon, it's an exciting and frenzied little beast which packs a lot into a short running time and features one of Downing's finest moments, as he's let off the leash to solo for all he's worth.

'Rock Hard Ride Free' (Tipton / Halford / Downing)

Priest didn't often complete a song and then leave it in the can. Often odd bits were recycled – 'Screaming For Vengeance' supposedly came to life via odds and ends from *Point Of Entry*, for example – but 'Rock Hard Ride Free' owes its heritage to an outtake from the *Screaming For Vengeance* sessions called 'Fight For Your Life'. Slower than the preceding neck-breakers it's a fine song which builds up to a glorious set of solos that showcase what Downing and Tipton can do when they work together before a subtle bridge swings things back into the song itself for the final verse, chorus and fade.

'The Sentinel' (Tipton / Halford / Downing)

On an album of fine songs, 'The Sentinel' still stands loud and proud as the best of the best of the best. The lyrics flow beautifully, describing The Sentinel of the title, a knife-throwing man with no name who's 'sworn to avenge' – so it looks like he's the good guy in this story of a standoff. As the cathedral bell ceases tolling his attackers advance, only to be cut down by the fearsome blades he despatches. OK, that doesn't read so well and fails to do the song justice on every count. 'The Sentinel' is pretty much perfect, an exquisitely paced song boasting perfect storytelling, atmosphere and a collection of polished performances from all concerned. If you had to pull together the band's best ever ten songs, this would have to be included. It is that simple.

'Love Bites' (Tipton / Halford / Downing)

Flipping the original album over, Side Two opens with the rather quirky 'Love Bites', one of those tracks like 'The Rage' which comes from left field and smacks you right in the face. A strong album cut whose live rendition redefines colossal, Priest's take on vampire lust is a terrific song whose false detuned bass intro gives way to a multi-layered masterpiece in which dramatic pauses add to the Hammer Horror style atmosphere. Onstage, Tipton comes in for the harmony vocals required in the second verse, but fortunately nothing else. The video shot for the song (which carries the album backing track but is shot in a semi-live manner) showcases the Metallian stage set that the album cover inspired, and a collectable 12" shaped disc issued in America is worth adding to your record collection should you ever come across it.

The song became the show opener for the tour – not the obvious choice, but a distinctive way to get an evening's Priest feast underway.

'Eat Me Alive' (Tipton / Halford / Downing)

Around this time the Parents Music Resource Center, an influential American pressure group led by Tipper Gore, began to flex its muscles in the argument over censorship. It pulled together its 'Filthy Fifteen', the 15 songs it most objected to. 'Eat Me Alive' came in at No.3, based on the rather literal interpretation of the words that it's about oral sex at gunpoint, although it could be no more than a continuation of Halford's forays into sexually supercharged lyricism. (Top of their list, for those who care, was Prince's 'Darling Nikki' and second came Sheena Easton's 'Sugar Walls', both being targeted because of their sexual themes. WASP's 'Animal (Fuck Like A Beast)' only made it to No.9.)

As a song 'Eat Me Alive' bounces along at a decent pace, and the alternating solos give it a bit of backbone, but it's probably the most throwaway song on the record and only breaks the three-and-a-half minute mark because no-one could be bothered to reach for the faders. Perhaps unsurprisingly, it was the only song that didn't make the live cut at some stage or another back in the day. Like many other lesser-achievers in the band's back catalogue, it finally made its live debut in 2008 when the band introduced to their set some lesser-known or new-to-the-stage songs from their back catalogue.

'Some Heads Are Gonna Roll' (R. Halligan Jr)

Priest's second song from the pen of Bob Halligan, Jnr was as commercially unsuccessful as its predecessor, despite having a much more interesting B-side, although unlike '(Take These) Chains' 'Some Heads Are Gonna Roll' did become a feature of the band's live set. It fits with the rest of the album's material admirably, but aside from earning Halligan some royalties, you really have to wonder what the band got out of the deal. *Defenders Of The Faith* is the sound of a band on a roll, and there's little doubt they could have come up with one more song of the necessary calibre without that much difficulty.

In the UK 'Some Heads Are Gonna Roll' was the album's second single, released in February 1984 and flipped with 'The Green Manalishi (With The Two-Pronged Crown)' and with the 12" adding 'Jawbreaker', meaning that out of three cuts on offer on that single only one was a band original. 'Jawbreaker' came straight off the album but with the sleeve only noting that 'The Green Manalishi…' was a live cut many people assumed it was the *Unleashed In the East* version and kept their wallets firmly in their pockets. It's actually lifted from the July 1981 New York Palladium show and is an excellent rendition from a recording which really should get an official release one day.

If you were quick, too, the 12" came with a Judas Priest stencil – surely a must for every-self-respecting fan – but this appears to have been, for once, a limited edition freebie in the true sense of the word and relatively hard to come by.

'Night Comes Down' (Tipton / Halford / Downing)

The album's token ballad is a sympathetic addition to the running order, imbued with a sense of power and purpose and featuring a great vocal performance from Halford. Geoff Barton's four-star review of *Defenders Of The Faith* in *Sounds* referred to this song as 'a remarkably good and moody ballad,

Halford flexing his vocal cords in a different direction and, by God, actually *singing* at one point.' It certainly is one of the album's many highlights.

It's an atmospheric and poignant track, which slows things down just a little before the album's coup de grâce. Live, 'Night Comes Down' was generally followed by the PA tape of 'The Hellion', meaning that Halford, in particular, could catch his breath once more before having to hit the highs of 'Electric Eye'.

'Heavy Duty' (Tipton / Halford / Downing)

'Heavy metal is probably one of the hardest styles of music to write,' Halford explained to Steve Gett, although 'Heavy Duty', another go at the 'Take On The World' vibe with crunching guitars and possibly a drum machine, is this album at its simplest. It doesn't really do much apart from give Halford the opportunity to menacingly snarl some lines in praise of the genre (and later give Downing a title for his autobiography), before giving way to…

'Defenders Of The Faith' (Tipton / Halford / Downing)

To be honest, the only reason this and 'Heavy Duty' are listed as two separate tracks is to increase the share of royalties. The one leads nicely into the other, and although 'Defenders Of The Faith' is only a one-and-a-half minute one-line singalong, it is a very good one-and-a-half minute one-line singalong. Between them 'Heavy Duty' and 'Defenders Of The Faith' fail to breach the four-minute mark, but there's something about the coupling that makes them pretty much the perfect ending to the perfect album.

Bizarrely, a number of writers at the time asked the band what faith they were defending, when you would have thought it was pretty damn obvious. 'Well, if you take the analysis of what the title means, instantly Priest are defenders of the faith,' Halford told Steve Gett in *Sounds*, 'the faith being heavy metal music. And we are defending it against every aspect: from the people that knock it, and from ever going out of style or fashion, which we never thought it would anyway. And so I think *Defenders Of The Faith* is apt, not only for Priest, but for all heavy metal freaks around the world. The fans and the bands – it's a statement for everybody.'

Post Album Events

With the Christmas decorations stowed away, the band brushed off their stage gear and appeared on Channel 4's music show The Tube on 6 January 1984, performing 'Electric Eye', 'Freewheel Burning', 'You've Got Another Thing Comin'' and 'Breaking The Law' before heading off to Europe for coffee and croissants and playing some 28 dates across the continent until 22 February. Just over three weeks later they were back in the States, treading the boards at the Niagara Falls Convention Centre on 16 March. It was only at this point that material from *Defenders Of The Faith* was fully integrated into the set, with the opening coupling of 'Love Bites' – as noted above, perhaps not the most exciting opener imaginable – and 'Jawbreaker' replacing 'The Hellion' / 'Electric Eye', although these would pop up later in the evening. By this time, only 'Sinner' and 'Victim Of Changes' remained in the set from the earlier days, with 'The Green Manalishi...' and 'Hell Bent For Leather' bringing the total of pre-1980 songs to just four. From the States, the band flew to Japan, and after a gig at the Budokan on 13 September paid their final hotel bills and made their way home.

The thirtieth-anniversary release of *Defenders Of The Faith* came with two bonus CDs showcasing the entire 104 minute live set recorded at Long Beach, California, on 5 May 1984. Rumours of a live release to capitalise on the success of *Defenders*... had been floating around, but instead, the band ploughed on with their next studio venture which didn't come easily and which restricted them to just one date – *Live Aid* (on the US stage, naturally) – in 1985. Whether this Long Beach recording would have been the source for a possible live album in 1985 is open to conjecture, but it would have kept things ticking over nicely while the musicians battled with their next venture, envisaged as an opulent double album entitled *Twin Turbos*.

Turbo (1986)

Personnel:
Rob Halford: lead vocals
Glenn Tipton: lead guitars
K.K. Downing: lead guitars
Ian Hill: bass
Dave Holland: drums
Record label:
Recorded at Compass Point Studios, Nassau, between June 1985 and February 1986
Produced by: Tom Allom
Release date: 14 April 1986
Highest chart positions: UK: 33, US: 17
Running time: 40:58

> *On 15 May 1986 I was in a record shop in Hammersmith, killing time before the doors opened at the Hammersmith Palais where Celtic Frost were due to play their first UK date, supported by fellow Noise Records acts Helloween and Grave Digger. With a shop full of metal fans, the guy at the counter changed records, and as the opening notes of 'Out In The Cold' drifted across the room a young metalhead shouted 'fuck off, Judas Priest!' and everybody cheered him. It was apparent that a changing of the guard was coming, and that the once-mighty Priest were, to many new metal fans, yesterday's men* – John Tucker, personal recollection

In April 1986 Rob Halford, K.K. Downing, Glenn Tipton, Ian Hill and Dave Holland delivered the most divisive and possibly most difficult album of their career. *Turbo* would go platinum in the States and give the band an equal Billboard chart placing with *Screaming For Vengeance*, whereas in the UK it stalled at just No.33 during a disappointing four-week run. Despite generally positive reviews in the UK music press to British ears it just didn't sound, well, Priest, and the old joke just after the album's release was that it had so far sold 500,000 thousand copies in America, and at least another four over here.

Turbo had a difficult birth. After the final night of the 1984 tour the band took a break from the road, and their only appearance in 1985 was their three-song set at Live Aid on 13 July ('Living After Midnight', 'The Green Manalishi (With The Two-Pronged Crown') and 'You've Got Another Thing Comin''). Downing reckons that the three songwriters rented a villa in Marbella around January 1985 to start throwing ideas around and that in this 'really creative time' they quickly amassed enough ideas for what would be a quite diverse double album. They even had a working title, *Twin Turbos*, inspired by the matching pair of Porsche 911 Turbo SEs the guitarists had purchased (Tipton's was white, Downing's black, trivia fans might care to know).

When they arrived at Compass Point Studios – or somewhere en route – the double album idea was ditched. In his autobiography, Downing reckoned that the band thought the idea unworkable, but double albums weren't all the rage in the Eighties and so it's possible that the record label's response was along the lines of 'no way, José'. As Halford told Matthias Mader at *Rock Hard* magazine in 2017:

> *We were in a great place at the time when we started writing the songs; we had a lot of ideas, a lot of enthusiasm. So when we got past the point of nine or ten songs, and we were still writing, we approached the label and said that what we'd like to do is make two releases and give them to the fans for the price of one release, but the label didn't like that idea at all! So as a result of that and other discussions we decided that we would condense the songs that we had into what was really the Turbo experience. The sound of the album would have changed quite dramatically had we included the rest of the material.*

So, as a result, the nineteen songs of *Twin Turbos* were whittled down to a nine-track collection, with some material being discarded, only to appear as bonus tracks, some left to languish in the vaults and the rest carried forward to *Ram It Down*. The songs that did make the final release were slick, sanitised and made for US FM radio – it's the perfect album to play in the car with the roof down under Californian skies: unfortunately, that didn't translate well to playing it on a Walkman on a bus on a cloudy day in Milton Keynes.

Halford meanwhile – and unbeknown to the rest of the band – was battling his own addiction to alcohol and cocaine. His partner at the time was also addicted and after a particularly tumultuous row shot himself dead in front of the singer. In January 1986 the singer checked himself into rehab, losing a month to getting himself clean once more. Downing too was going through a particularly messy split with his long-term partner, although as he admits he was barely able to keep his trousers on for more than about five minutes when he was on tour or recording in sunnier climes, so sympathy for him is hard to come by. And then there was the Top Gun fiasco…

But in the midst of all of this *Turbo* was delivered and, as noted above, became a bestseller across the Atlantic and a much-derided relic in the UK – even Doug Johnson's futuristic, multi-coloured gear stick cover art was lampooned as an ice cream. The UK critics liked it, though. In fact, they were overwhelmingly gushing about Priest's tenth studio album. 'OK, so let's not pussy-foot around here, guys, this is it!! Wimps move aside, AOR fans run for cover – this is Real Man's music, accept no substitute; the kings of heavy metal are back at their greatest, Earth-splintering, toe-nail removing best!!' said Dave Dickson in *Kerrang!* Meanwhile, over at Metal Forces, Garry Sharpe wrote:

> *The ignition track is heavier than the sky falling on your head, growling thunder by Glenn and storm clouds/lightning courtesy of K.K. The production excels, the hammer is down all the way, and that's where it stays for the duration… The breaks are sharper and faster (Ken has his*

> *greatest moment yet on 'Reckless'), the drums are piled on and at last Rob's vocals have been given more priority than on previous outings. Even so, it's all very, very commercial (cue baboon chorus of 'sell out!') but so f**king what??! Priest will never rehash* Sin After Sin *again, so there's no point in bitching.*

It doesn't help that the album wasn't toured in their native land, the usual excuse trotted out was that the expansive stage set was too big for British venues, although at least the tour did take in a handful of European dates this time. But was the album a blatant stab at the massive US market? The band made no secret, in interviews, of their disappointment at not achieving the same sales as some of their peers, and must have been astounded when Def Leppard's hugely contrived *Hysteria* swept all before it the following year. Or perhaps it was an attempt to break free of the (largely self-imposed) shackles of traditional metal music. They could easily have recorded *Screaming…3* and watched it sell quite well but had they created the varied, sprawling double album they'd originally envisaged, it might have been their *Sergeant Pepper* rather than their Dr Pepper.

Of the *Twin Turbo* tracks that didn't make the final selection four – 'Ram It Down', 'Hard As Iron', 'Love You To Death' and 'Monsters Of Rock' became an integral part of the band's next album. Another four would be used as bonus tracks for the 2001 re-issues. The execrable 'Red, White And Blue' was added to *British Steel*, 'Prisoner Of Your Eyes' to *Screaming For Vengeance*, 'Turn On Your Light' to *Defenders Of The Faith* and 'All Fired Up' was reunited with its bedfellows on the *Turbo* revamp. 'Under The Gun' and 'Fighting For Your Love' remain unreleased and 'Heart Of A Lion', listed as a 'previously unreleased demo', cropped up on the 2004 *Metalogy* box set, although it had rather surprisingly already appeared on Racer X's 1987 album Second Heat. Living in Phoenix, Arizona, Halford had become friends with Racer X's singer Jeff Martin, and gifted him the song, as he explained to Matthias Mader:

> *It was just one track out of the extra material that was floating around, and we were good friends with the band Racer X, in fact, I believe Scott Travis was in the band at the time. It was just a gesture that was made so that they could give it their own interpretation. And then a little bit later I recorded it separately with the Halford band.*

The song appeared again on Racer X's second live album *Extreme Volume II Live* which appeared posthumously in September 1992, by which time, of course, Travis was a fully-fledged member of Judas Priest. Life can certainly be peculiar at times.

'Turbo Lover' (Tipton / Halford / Downing)

Boasting one of the most recognisable intros since Deep Purple's 'Fireball' the album's opening song and *de facto* title track is a masterclass of pacing and development, building from a very simple opening verse into a powerful, muscle-bound pugilist. It also sets out the band's new approach from the off, and some long-term fans had already made up their minds that this really wasn't the album for them before Tipton's solo had kicked in.

The guitarists had been messing around with Roland synth guitars since they'd had a guided tour of the Hamer factory a couple of years earlier. Sat around in Marbella, Downing recalled that:

> *One day Glenn plugged in and played us a sound that resembled an aircraft taking off. Or maybe a turbocharger spooling up.*
> *'Hold on. Play that again,' Rob said.*
> *'You mean this?' Whhhhaaaowwwwwoooossssssh!*
> *'Yes, that.'*

Downing noted that he wouldn't claim that 'the sound informed the whole writing process, but it was definitely significant … We never for a moment questioned whether the guitar synth fit [sic] into Judas Priest.'

'Turbo Lover' is a clever song, in fact, it's a great song, but it made a lousy single, even supported by a ridiculously camp sci-fi themed video to tie in with (or maybe explain) the band's new made-to-measure outfits. Released in April, it sank without a trace. Both 7" and 12" versions carried companion album track 'Hot For Love' on the flip, and although the 12" proudly proclaimed itself to be the 'Extended Version' at 5:24 it was just the full album version, rather than the 7" and video edit. Reviewing the single for *Kerrang!* Dave Dickson was so excitable that he wrote the whole review in block capitals 'so that you can get an inkling of the sheer mega-heaviosity in which we're engaged here.' It was, in his opinion, 'completely and utterly brilliant and totally great.'

Of much more interest is the 'Turbo Hi-Octane Mix' which first put in an appearance on the European 'Parental Guidance' 12" release, a seven-and-a-half minute (near as dammit) vaguely annoying club remix attributed to The Hellion Kid. Given the response to the album in the UK, it's a good job this wasn't made available over here at the time as it really would have put the cat amongst Priest's pigeons. It would finally appear in 1998 on the *Priest, Live And Rare* CD, a collection of live B-sides with this 'gem' tacked on at the end.

'Locked In' (Tipton / Halford / Downing)

The second track on the album would go on to be the second single drawn from it, with an even more ridiculous video although one which continued the storyline of 'Turbo Lover'. Such as it is. Perfectly placed as the album's second track 'Locked In' upped the ante somewhat, taking the power of 'Turbo Lover' and galloping along in a similar fashion to 'Riding On The Wind'. Another love song – given Halford's recent relationship difficulties it's perhaps unsurprising that many of the album's lyrics are more grounded, and revolve around the realities of life – and Halford delivers his lyrics as the love-sick Lothario with great assurance. Meanwhile, the band deliver a cast-iron riff and a clever split solo during which at gigs the singer would strut between the guitarists.

US record-buyers would see the single backed by 'Hot For Love' while in the UK the 7" version was twinned with 'Reckless' while the 12" again featured an 'extended version' (which again was just the album track) plus a fold-out 36" x 24" poster of the band in all their *Turbo*-era glory. In truth, the image has been enlarged far beyond its means and looks terribly grainy, but, hey, it was free. The package also included two live tracks, 'Desert Plains' and 'Free Wheel Burning' [sic], from the Long Beach, California, show on 5 May 1984.

'Private Property' (Tipton / Halford / Downing)

Ignoring the synth intro, 'Private Property' could be cut from the same cloth as *Bloodstone* – not a great song, certainly, but one which happily plods along to its vocally multi-layered chorus. The guitars cut through nicely, another Tipton solo sits comfortably within the framework, and you have to wonder whether this was the single that should have been taken from the album rather than the preceding cuts. Instead, a live version taken from the gig taped at Kiel Auditorium, St Louis, Missouri on 23 May 1986 appeared as the flip to the European 12" release of 'Parental Guidance', alongside the 'Turbo Lover' remix.

'Parental Guidance' (Tipton / Halford / Downing)

Having been in the gunsights of Tipper Gore's Parents Music Resource Centre, who wanted 'parental advisory' stickers labelling any record that had violent, or sexual, or drug-related themes – basically anything that wasn't fluffy, wholesome and American – Priest hit back by taking their 'parental guidance' phrase and turning it into a semi-comedic verbal dispute between the cool and the straight. Or it could be taken as a battle of the generations, although as Gore was only three years older than Halford that doesn't work in the context of the PMRC. It's a fun song, not to be taken too seriously, despite the leverage the PMRC had at the time, and lyrically rather clever. It's not the greatest thing the band have ever written, but then nor is 'Breaking The Law'. And, to round off the song's message of living for the moment, the opening line of 'You've Got Another Thing Comin'' was cleverly dropped in.

'Rock You All Around The World' (Tipton / Halford / Downing)

Even the most battle-hardened defender of some of Priest's less worthy outings would be hard-pressed to find a good thing to say about this one. It's relatively short, which is, I guess, a positive. It's a throwaway piece of bubblegum metal designed to get the crowd going with its singalong chorus and absolutely terrible lyrics which I don't suppose Halford spent much time pontificating over. It was singled out in *Metal Forces* most embarrassingly. ''Rock You All Around The World' is crap,' wrote Garry Sharpe. 'The lead break saves it – just. Charity doesn't extend to letting your granny write the odd ditty for you, Rob.'

'Out In The Cold' (Tipton / Halford / Downing)

The longest song on the album – in fact, the longest song from the band since 'Beyond The Realms Of Death' – 'Out In The Cold' is a beautifully crafted mid-paced long song which features exceptional performances from all concerned. Perhaps surprisingly, as it's not what you'd call an attention grabber, it would go on to become the opening song of the band's set for the forthcoming tour. Halford's melodramatic plaintive cry 'where are you now?' resonates with the lost and the lonely, and the whole song is a heart-breaking delight, a whisper in the dark.

Far too synthesiser-orientated for many of the hardcore fans to swallow, 'Out In The Cold' can hold its head high in the pantheon of great songs the band have produced over the years, and an edit would surely have made another potential single. But then, what do I know?

'Wild Nights, Hot And Crazy Days' (Tipton / Halford / Downing)

The clunky title – it's not exactly 'Sinner', is it? – gives way to a clunky song of little joy or merit. The fact that *Kerrang!* gave the album a five-out-of-five write-up yet this is the only song reviewer Dave Dickson failed to talk about says it all. The drums thump metronomically, the synths tap away, and although Halford still sings it like his life depends on it, and Downing turns in a very metal solo, this is turgid.

'Hot For Love' (Tipton / Halford / Downing)

Another piece of fun 'n' fluff 'Hot For Love' does push its Eighties production in your face a little too much, particularly with those annoying synthesised drum sounds more at home in a nightclub or a trendy boutique than on a metal album. Probably *Turbo*'s least interesting song – and certainly one which hasn't aged gracefully.

'Reckless' (Tipton / Halford / Downing)

Things take a turn for the better with 'Reckless' which is a fine way to wrap the album up. 'Reckless' is again rather mid-paced, and perhaps a distant relative of 'You've Got Another Thing Comin'' or maybe 'Rock Hard, Ride Free' with a staunch riff and plenty of might. Like much of the album it's hugely accessible, and its simplicity gives it a kind of cranial staying power: once you've heard the song, it stays in your head for days on end. And unlike the majority of the album it's not a long song but one which lives for the street: it's young, it's cocky, it's streetwise, and so it was felt to be the perfect fit for the soundtrack for a new film called Top Gun starring a relative newcomer called Tom Cruise. The band had to decide whether to give away one of the record's finest songs and potentially unbalance the album (although presumably, they could still have worked up one of the *Twin Turbo* leftovers) or just ignore the offer. They reckoned that the film would probably stiff anyway so passed on the deal. History would, unfortunately, show that Top Gun would go on to gross $180 million or thereabouts and that the original soundtrack album would be one of the biggest selling OSTs of all time. If life is like a box of chocolates, sometimes you get there to find someone's already scoffed the lot…

Post Album Events

Touring in support of the album – the *Fuel For Life* trek – began on 2 May 1986 at Tingley Coliseum, Albuquerque, and ran through the summer, the American and Canadian leg of the tour wrapping up on 31 August in Toronto. Along the way, at least four gigs were recorded: Sandstone Amphitheater, Bonner Springs, Kansas show on 22 May; Kiel Auditorium, Saint Louis, Missouri on 23 May; The Omni, Atlanta, Georgia on 15 June; and Reunion Arena, Dallas, on 27 June. *Kerrang!*'s Derek Oliver reviewed the show at the Sports Arena, Los Angeles (11 or 12 May – they played two nights at that venue) noting that 'Judas Priest now boast the biggest stage set I have ever seen,' and that 'the audience were treated to a constant whirling spectacle that reverberated to a choice selection of material covering most of Priest's long and varied career.' The full expanse of the show would be unveiled via the *Priest…Live!* video the following year. Oliver also, however, revealed that Legs Diamond drummer Jonathan Valen was sat behind the scenes, apparently playing the drums in Holland's stead. A hasty communiqué from the band's management pointed out that all Valen did was supply some assistance with some of the effects triggers. It was all a bit of a non-story, really, but Oliver called Holland 'a drummer with nowhere new to go' which can't have been much of a confidence boost for the band's longest-serving tub-thumper.

After a short break, European dates commenced on 28 September in Zwolle in The Netherlands and seeing the sights of Germany, Spain, Switzerland and Scandinavia kept the lads occupied till the end of October. Then it was off to Japan at the start of December, and a final gig in Honolulu on 16 December brought the curtain down once more. Nothing from *Turbo* would be played in the UK until the band were filmed and recorded at a one-off at the Brixton Academy in London on 19 December 2001, when the Ripper Owens line-up belted out 'Turbo Lover'. Bizarrely, the crowd went absolutely wild!

1987 would see the band play even fewer dates than 1985 while they concentrated on a new record. As for *Turbo*, it was the final album – to date, at least – to be given a thirtieth-anniversary makeover. The simply-named *Turbo 30* appeared in 2017 (OK, a tad late) and was padded out with a two-CD set featuring the entire show from the Sandstone Amphitheater, Bonner Springs, Kansas show on 22 May. The four-panel fold-out cardboard CD case features a photo of each band member by photographer Mark Weiss at the time of the 'Turbo Lover' video shoot although the one absentee is disgraced drummer Dave Holland, who'd been conveniently forgotten by the time of the release.

Priest... Live! (1987)

Personnel:
Rob Halford: vocals
Glenn Tipton: lead guitars
K.K. Downing: lead guitars
Ian Hill: bass
Dave Holland: drums
Record label: CBS
Recorded live at: The Omni, Atlanta, Georgia, 15 June 1986, and Reunion Arena, Dallas, 27 June 1986
Produced by: Tom Allom
Release date: 28 May 1987
Highest chart positions: UK: 47, US: 38
Running time: 74:00

> *The essence of Judas Priest is great metal music. They really try hard to deliver the goods, if you know what I mean, they really try hard to come up with stuff that their fans will like, and 99.9% of the time they really hit the mark, bang on* – Biff Byford, Saxon

Given the success of the band's previous three albums in America, particularly *Turbo*, it's little surprise that their second live album would be drawn from the US dates of the *Fuel For Life* tour. There is no doubt that the tour was a spectacle – the robot's appearance as 'The Hellion' tape rolls is nothing short of amazing – and it's still beyond belief to this day that although Judas Priest spent so much time on the road they didn't play any British dates at all. Even K.K. Downing admits that 'we should have toured the UK' when asked about it.

As with its predecessor *Priest... Live!* was culled from the best of two nights, this time The Omni, Atlanta, Georgia on 15 June 1986 and the Reunion Arena, Dallas, 27 June 1986, and came as a double live spectacular, with just a few numbers edited out to fit four sides of vinyl. The cover was, however, terrible, and the inner of the gatefold even worse, boasting a great live shot, not dissimilar to the spectacle that is *Kiss's Alive II*, with superimposed hands stretching out. File under awful.

A live video followed in September shot entirely at the Dallas show. This, of course, wasn't the first live show the band had released as that honour had gone to the stunningly-titled *Judas Priest Live*, filmed at the Mid South Coliseum, Memphis, Tennessee, on 12 December 1982 and put out the following year. *The Priest... Live!* video resurrected the tracks lost because of the limitations of vinyl, but for some reason kicked 'Metal Gods' into touch with just a snippet used over the closing credits; and final encore 'Hell Bent For Leather' was edited so that alongside the footage of the song were highlights of the rest of the show so as to make a 'best of' video clip for the purposes of MTV. It would have been better to have kept the original footage intact, and then also included this edited version as a bonus track. But what do I know?

So, putting everything together, this is what was presented for fans' audio and / or visual delight: 'Out In The Cold' / 'Locked In' [video only] / 'Heading Out To The Highway' / 'Metal Gods' [LP only] / 'Breaking The Law' / 'Love Bites' / 'Some Heads Are Gonna Roll' / 'The Sentinel' / 'Private Property' / 'Desert Plains' [video only] / 'Rock You All Around The World' / 'The Hellion' / 'Electric Eye' / 'Turbo Lover ' / 'Freewheel Burning' / 'The Green Manalishi (With The Two-Pronged Crown)' [video only] / 'Parental Guidance' / 'Living After Midnight' / 'You've Got Another Thing Comin'' / 'Hell Bent For Leather' [video only]

It's apparent that, aside from 'Hell Bent For Leather' there's nothing pre-1980 in the set, although 'Victim Of Changes' did put in an appearance during the tour and is captured on the Sandstone Amphitheater, Bonner Springs, Kansas show on 22 May which came (much later) as the bonus discs with *Turbo 30*.

Whether you like *Turbo* or not, this is a fine collection of songs – 'Rock You All Around The World' aside – and the performances are straight from the top drawer. Although most of the songs are played pretty straight, 'Heading Out To The Highway' features a solo apiece from Downing and Tipton before the usual dual licks, and 'Breaking The Law' also gives Downing another brief moment in the spotlight. Tipton meanwhile gets the chance to flex his muscles as part of the intro to the Harley-hogging 'Hell Bent For Leather'.

'Judas Priest played a huge part in our musical development,' notes Raven's John Gallagher, who in 1976 had come across a review of *Sad Wings Of Destiny* 'christening K.K. as a "proto flash feedback screamer" and touting Halford's amazing voice' and immediately bought it. 'I loved it and drove all my mates nuts – and made them Priest fans! And then we saw them at Newcastle Mayfair in 1977 where the first song was 'Call For The Priest'. Just brutal!' he laughs. Little did he know that not only would his band buy Priest's *Screaming For Vengeance* stage set, but that less than ten years later Raven would be opening for them.

We did five dates on the Turbo *tour. We played with them in Albuquerque, New Mexico; Denver, Colorado; Salt Lake City, Los Angeles (Irvine Meadows) and San Diego [so the very first dates of the tour, in May 1986]. They were all very friendly, very gracious; I remember Glenn and K.K. sitting there, talking to us about the evils of certain promoters. Rob – our Rob [Hunter – drummer] – was very drunk and getting in the way of everything, but Rob Halford was very quiet but friendly, Ian Hill, friendly, Dave Holland, friendly ... They were great. And the crew loved us, they just said, 'whatever you do, just don't break any of our shit. Do whatever you want. Full lights, full sound, go for it.'*

Turbo *was very much a similar thing to what we'd been doing, so we understood the difficulties around crowd acceptance. OK, so some*

> *of the lyrics were a little on the cheesy side, but I've thought the same about some of our albums! Live it was great, especially the second night. They were watching us, and it was great because we were on, we were playing really good, and it upped their game, you could see they upped their game, and I love it when that happens. I love a little bit of friendly competition. And they went out, and they nailed it. Halford was great, he was singing at the top of his game.*

Most people assumed that when *Priest… Live!* was given its 2001 makeover the missing video tracks would be re-instated. The record company thought otherwise though, adding two tracks completely unconnected to the *Fuel For Life* tour – 'Screaming For Vengeance' from the *Judas Priest Live* video and 'Rock Hard, Ride Free' from the 5 May 1984 Long Beach, California set. At least the third bonus cut did have some relevance, being a cracking version of 'Hell Bent For Leather' recorded at Kiel Auditorium, Saint Louis, Missouri on 23 May 1986.

Ram It Down (1988)

Personnel:
Rob Halford: lead vocals
Glenn Tipton: lead guitars
K.K. Downing: lead guitars
Ian Hill: bass guitar
Dave Holland: drums
Record label: CBS
Recorded at: Ibiza Sound Studios, Spain, and Puk Studios, Denmark December 1987 – March 1988
Produced by: Tom Allom
Release date: 17 May 1988
Highest chart positions: UK: 24, US: 31
Running time: 49:33

> *I wouldn't exactly describe it as an era of confusion, but we were uncertain about the future. I can remember talking to the guys and [manager] Bill Curbishley and saying I was unhappy. My departure from the band wasn't spontaneous; it had been brewing since about 1986*
> – Rob Halford in *Classic Rock Presents Heavy Metal*

It's fair to say that if Rob Halford, K.K. Downing, Glenn Tipton, Ian Hill and Dave Holland had one shot at being a multi-million selling band, racking up sales in the same ballpark as Def Leppard's *Hysteria*, Whitesnake's *1987* or Quiet Riot's *Metal Health*, *Turbo* was it. By definition, you only ever get one once-in-a-lifetime opportunity, and in terms of global mega-sales, and with the luxury of hindsight, Priest blew it. Sales and chart placings from that point on would be no more than 'respectable' for a band of their stature, and UK tours would be of 'decent-sized' venues. It wasn't over, by any stretch of the imagination: it wasn't the beginning of the end, but it was certainly the end of the beginning. After *Ram It Down*, the band would part company with both Holland and producer Tom Allom as they searched for a new direction which, in turn, would see them flounder for a decade. The band wouldn't work with Allom again until he hooked up with them once more to co-produce 2009's *A Touch Of Evil: Live* album, exactly thirty years after he'd first sat at his console with the tapes of *Unleashed In The East* before him. His next studio credit with the band wouldn't come until 2018's *Firepower* album. The artwork came from a new set of brushes as well, as after three covers by Doug Johnson *Ram It Down* featured an illustration by Mark Wilkinson, familiar to many through his work with Marillion, whose work would go on to adorn several other Priest sleeves.

To call *Ram It Down* a mess would be an insult to teenagers' bedrooms across the land. OK, so that might be a little far from the truth, but it is unfocused and muddled, and you have to wonder if the band were throwing ideas at the studio wall just to see what stuck. Yet it must have been a relatively productive exercise, in quantity if not in quality. Although four songs had been carried forward from the *Turbo* sessions, the band came up with five new compositions and generated another three songs which remained in storage once the album was complete. On the other hand, the album also included their take on 'Johnny B Goode', their worst ever cover version, and possibly the worst idea ever in the history of bad ideas. To be fair to *Ram It Down*, it did considerably better in the UK charts than *Turbo*, peaking at No.24 in a five-week run, compared to *Turbo*'s highest placing of No.33 with just four weeks basking in the national spotlight, but that's no more than damning it with faint praise. '*Ram It Down* is not one of my favourite Judas Priest albums really. In fact, I don't think it's anybody's favourite, to be honest!' laughed producer Tom Allom when discussing it with *Rock Hard*'s Matthias Mader in 2018.

The scope of the 'what exactly are we doing here?' confusion, is perhaps best exemplified by the band's decision to collaborate with Mike Stock, Matt Aitken and Pete Waterman, better known for churning out poptastic hits for the likes of Mel & Kim, Bananarama, Dead Or Alive and Roland Rat. The whole thing was supposedly done at Halford's request, and with the bulk of *Ram It Down* in the can Priest flew to Paris where they recorded three songs – two SAW originals ('Runaround' and 'I Will Return') and a cover of Stylistics' 1971 hit 'You Are Everything'. Halford remains proud of the work whereas the rest of the band seem happy that the tracks have been buried (although there is a snippet of 'You Are Everything' on the internet: it sounds like anything you find in supermarkets on CDs with titles like Now That's What I Call Best Metal Ballads Ever 27). Whereas it's possible that the metal fraternity might have embraced Judas Priest working with pop producers – even ones with such a cachet as Stock, Aitken and Waterman – in truth it is extremely unlikely, and, let's be fair, coming after *Turbo* the band would have been crucified. What was I saying about the worst idea in the history of bad ideas? That Halford still feels that working with Stock, Aitken and Waterman was worth investigating and that the results were meaningful is perhaps an indication of his growing restlessness within the confines of the band, although it would take a while yet for this to come to a head.

'Ram It Down' (Tipton / Halford / Downing)

The first of the four tracks which could have appeared on *Twin Turbos*, the album's title track arrives in explosive fashion – no preamble, no fluff, just a piercing scream and bang! – in come guitars, drums and bass in a battery of pure power. 'Ram It Down' follows in the raw tradition of in-your-face openers, and answers the question 'what would happen if you could genetically splice 'Exciter' and 'Rapid Fire'. It's essentially a minute-and-a-half intricate and exciting dual guitar solo which shouts loud and proud 'we're back' encased in a song. The lyrical delivery is as frenetic (and as throwaway) as they come for a heads-down juggernaut and 'bodies revving in leather heaven in wonder/lights are dimmin' and heads are swimming as thunder hits the stage' is as good as anything else Halford has delivered with his tongue firmly in his cheek over the years .

OK, the pre-solo bridge is a bit wussy, but overall 'Ram It Down' was a statement of intent, a song designed to expunge any doubts naysayers might have had about the album.

'Heavy Metal' (Tipton / Halford / Downing)

Quite surprisingly, a Tipton solo sets the scene, but after nary a beat the drums, bass and vocals introduce the album's second song, the self-explanatory 'Heavy Metal'. From the off Priest were a band synonymous with metal and they never ducked this tag even when the genre was routinely disparaged throughout the late Seventies and early Eighties, so it comes as no great revelation that a song with such a simplistic yet heartfelt title would pop up somewhere along the line. The result is a medium-paced neck-breaker, and the song (like 'Ram It Down') made it into the live set for the duration of the tour. At close on six minutes, this is the album's second longest cut, but a good 45 seconds is Tipton widdling away and doing his thing. You have to wonder how, given the developing enmity between the two guitarists, Downing might have felt about his opposite number getting such a chance to show off.

'Love Zone' (Tipton / Halford / Downing)

Priest get funky and get down! Another song from the cabinet marked 'left field' and driven by a pounding drum pattern 'Love Zone' hops and skips along like a schoolkid on holiday, and although there's not a great deal of substance to it, it is (a) a little different for the band and (b) has an innate charm which is hard to criticise. Furthermore, it's enlivened by another split and dual solo, and if you're really still not convinced, it's the joint shortest song on offer and so doesn't overstay its welcome.

'Come And Get It' (Tipton / Halford / Downing)

Unfortunately, things now start to go downhill. 'Do you like it heavy / Do you love it mean / Do you want it dirty / We don't play it clean,' sneers Halford over a track which could easily have been one of *Turbo*'s low spots, although it was actually a new cut, albeit a bit of a ploddy filler which screams drum machine. 'It's fairly common knowledge on the *Ram It Down* album that we didn't actually use a drummer,' Tom Allom would tell Matthias Mader years later. Halford takes it seriously – in fact, he's on top form throughout the album – but there's little of any great note going on here. It did actually make the live set, generally as part of an early pairing of songs from the new album with 'I'm A Rocker' following it, although that doesn't really mean it's any good.

'Hard As Iron' (Tipton / Halford / Downing)

Laden with annoying and obtrusive sound effects and little else of note, 'Hard As Iron' could have rubbed shoulders with 'Come And Get It' as another of *Turbo*'s potential nadirs, being the second of the *Twin Turbos* hand-me-downs. It is what it is, which isn't saying much, and it isn't really the band's finest four minutes. C'mon guys; you can do better than this.

'Blood Red Skies' (Tipton / Halford / Downing)

The opening cut on Side Two again sounds like it could have been on *Turbo* but again, despite the synths, this is another new offering. A science fantasy offering of the outsider evading the authorities, 'Blood Red Skies' is a powerful, atmospheric piece of storytelling in the vein of 'The Sentinel' which up to this point *Ram It Down* has sadly missed. Slowly unveiling itself over almost eight minutes 'Blood Red Skies' is majestic and erudite and shows that the band's well of creativity was yet to run dry. Downing has probably his finest moment on this album, and Halford breathes fierce determination and defiance into the lyrics.

The problem though is by now apparent as you get the distinct impression that the songwriters don't know whether the album is *Screaming For Vengeance* 3 or *Turbo* 2 and the new *Ram It Down* material collectively sits uneasily on the fence between the two.

'I'm A Rocker' (Tipton / Halford / Downing)

It's worth approaching any song entitled 'I'm A Rocker' – no matter who it's by – with a modicum of caution. This is terrible. Not since the tail end of *Point Of Entry* have the band served up something so completely meaningless. Again, they must have liked it sufficiently to include it in their live set, although most nights it was probably drowned out by the sound of several hundred toilets flushing at once.

'Johnny B. Goode' (Berry)

Although 'Ram It Down' was released as a single in mainland Europe, the sole UK single was this appallingly bad Chuck Berry cover. The 7" version came in a lovely gatefold sleeve, and that's about the best you can say for it, really. With seemingly no great interest in commercial success – although maybe someone mistakenly thought it was good enough to sell on its own merit – it was backed by 'Rock You All Around the World' with the 12" adding 'Turbo Lover', both from the recent *Priest... Live!* album. This was the band's first single to appear on CD but came in the short-lived 3" version, with 'Living After Midnight' (again from the 1987 live album) making up the running time.

After completely missing the boat with the 'Reckless' / Top Gun fiasco the band weren't looking to turn down another movie tie-in, so when the opportunity to submit a track for a film called Johnny Be Good they recorded the Chuck Berry classic. What? You must remember the film? According to IMDb this goofy comedy cost $22 million and grossed $5m in its opening weekend in the States, eventually losing in the region of $5 million overall. The soundtrack album also featured Kix, Ted Nugent, Saga and other such rock luminaries, but that didn't help either. Both film and OST sank without a trace. It's worth noting that, although the song is 'Johnny B. Goode', the single sleeve shows it as 'Johnny Be Good' and uses the same logo as the film posters.

Given that there are three known outtakes from *Ram It Down*, including this track on the album was a really bad move. To its credit it did tickle the lower reaches of the UK singles charts, peaking at No.64 in a two-week run, but the band didn't even bother including it in their 2011 Single Cuts box set of replica CD singles. This might have been related to copyright as the single (like the OST) was released on Atlantic Records, or simply because some nightmares just should not be revisited. The song was played live on the early European dates but certainly by the time they'd reached the UK it had been ditched. Thankfully.

'Love You To Death' (Tipton / Halford / Downing)

The album runs off with two final offerings from the *Twin Turbos* concept, the first being another outing from the S&M closet. Opening with the crack of a whip and ending, thankfully, just four-and-a-half minutes later 'Love You To Death', despite Halford's interesting vocal inflexion, is the B-side that never was. Rather like *Killing Machine*'s closing cut 'Love You To Death' does pick up the pace for the final minute or thereabouts, and in fact 'Evil Fantasies' does form the template for 'Love You To Death'. Unfortunately, though, the band did it much better the first time around.

'Monsters Of Rock' (Tipton / Halford / Downing)

And so this unconvincing album closes with one of those epics that promises much and delivers little. In bucketloads. This self-referential piece – the monster of rock of the title, born of the Black Country, is, of course, the mighty Priest – is completely and utterly worthless. Opening with the monster stomp of this monster of rock the song is wholly unconvincing lyrically, and musically the excitement level never rises above flatlining. Despite a half-way decent solo, 'Monsters Of Rock' plods along with all the grace of a beached whale. On the plus side, it is nicely produced, and the 2001 remaster does give it (as with much of the material on *Ram It Down*) a real punch, but five-and-a-half minutes after the song started it's all over, leaving you bewildered and wondering exactly what the point was.

Post Album Events

Once again, with usual disorganisation associated with Judas Priest and gigging vs releases, the tour started on 7 May in Stockholm, so the first eight dates were played before the new album was actually available to buy. It was, however, a lengthy slog that kept them living out of suitcases until the tail end of October and which took them across continental Europe and thence to the UK, Canada and America. It was preceded by a short visit to the Roxy Club in Amsterdam on 3 April where a handful of songs were played to a small audience invited to witness the filming of the video clip for 'Johnny B. Goode'. As mentioned above, four of the album's ten songs made the live set, played in pairs with 'Come And Get It' and 'Heavy Metal' appearing early in the set and 'Ram It Down' and 'I'm A Rocker' coming in the second half. 'Johnny B Goode' was served up as the first encore for a number of the early shows.

Seemingly desperate to make amends for ignoring the UK for four-and-a-half years Priest opened the UK leg of the tour with a date at Birmingham's

Powerhouse on 12 June and played a further eight dates (including two nights at Hammersmith Odeon) in theatre-sized venues. The support band was to have been Cinderella, but as they were struggling to complete their second album, *Long Cold Winter*, Bonfire got the nod, with Cinderella joining the tour later and Slayer picking up the last thirteen dates across America. The show opened with the familiar, 'The Hellion' tape rolling and then the band crashing in with 'Electric Eye' like it was 1982, although on both the dates I saw Halford sort of ambled on midway through the first verse rather than appearing behind a curtain of flash bombs, thus robbing the intro of some of its effect. The set itself really was a mixed bag and relied on some well-loved and highly respected crowd pleasers, so the four newbies rubbed shoulders with the likes of 'Sinner', 'Victim Of Changes' and even 'Beyond The Realms Of Death' was back in the show for the first time since the *Point Of Entry* tour in 1981. Paul Miller witnessed one of the Hammersmith shows for *Kerrang!*:

> *The stage show, in sharp contrast to the last US extravaganza, was extremely modest: an almost unnoticeable drum-riser flanked by a bank of amps and topped with a simple walkway. But it was the lighting that made the show, sacrificing a cumbersome and moving rig for an effective combination of mobile lights and highly responsive colour changing spots... 'Victim of Changes' transformed the upper balcony into a mass of flaying hair, and Fleetwood Mac's 'Green Manalishi' brought the set to a stylish conclusion, the Hammersmith choir eagerly helping Rob out at the death. Naturally, the ever-present Harley was rolled out to help the third and final encore, the tried and trusted 'Well Bent For Trevor'... From the moment the lights dimmed to the final Tipton 'n' Downing guitars-crossed salute from atop the walkway, Judas Priest never faltered. No sticky moments, a plethora of peaks and enough camp humour to fuel a generation of dodgy sit-coms. Simply, Priest put on the best metal show since Slayer last bulldozed into town, and were worth every damn second of the five-year wait.*

Nothing from the album survived to appear on the next tour though, and nor did Dave Holland, the band's longest-serving drummer by a mile at that point. His departure has never been fully explained, but the fact that after the best part of nine years with the band he was still on a wage must have rankled.

Despite the fact that the *Ram It Down* sessions yielded three outtakes, the 2001 re-issue veered away from the norm and was augmented by two live tracks rather than the usual one-live-one-studio-cut template. Although no dates were included in the booklet, 'Night Comes Down' was recorded at the Long Beach, California, show on 5 May 1984, while 'Bloodstone' came from the *Judas Priest Live* video filmed at Mid South Coliseum, Memphis, Tennessee, 12 December 1982. The fact that they are conjoined is mere studio trickery. As for the album's actual outtakes, 'Thunder Road' was added to the re-issue of *Point Of Entry* and 'Fire Burns Below' was donated to *Stained Class*. 'My

Design' remains unissued. Rumour has it that 'Thunder Road' was bunked from *Ram It Down* by 'Johnny B. Goode', and there is a degree of similarity to the two songs if you listen carefully. Given that 'Thunder Road' isn't a bad song, and looking back with the safety of many years of water under the bridge, it would have been much better to have left the single off the album altogether and allowed 'Thunder Road' to have kept its place in the running order.

Meanwhile, backstage at the Lawlor Events Centre in Reno, Nevada, on 30 September the band had been astonished to be served a subpoena and discover that they were being sued for their part in the death of two young fans.

Priest On Trial

Up to this point in time 'Better By You, Better Than Me' – the late addition to *Stained Class* which the people at CBS thought would be a hit – was no more than one of many songs in the band's back catalogue. However, it would go on to achieve a wholly unwanted new-found notoriety when it was the focus of a court case brought by the families of two American fans.

On 23 December 1985 twenty-year-old Ray Belknap and his eighteen-year-old friend James Vance entered into a suicide pact. Having listened to *Stained Class*, drunk and high on dope, Belknap put a shotgun under his chin and blew his head off. Vance reloaded, but his hands slipped on the blood-covered weapon as he pulled the trigger. He survived the incident but was terribly disfigured, and died of a drug overdose three years later. He memorably claimed that "alcohol and heavy metal music, such as Judas Priest, led us or even 'mesmerised' us into believing that the answer to life is death..."

Having been served on 30 September 1988 Rob Halford, K.K. Downing, Glenn Tipton and Ian Hill appeared in court for the first time on 16 July 1990. The accusation was that the track 'Better By You, Better Than Me' contained a subliminal message 'do it!' which urged those who heard it to commit suicide. Evidence for this was that both men were heard to chant the phrase before the shootings. Despite the fragility (and possibly stupidity) of such an argument, the prosecution made further allegations, claiming that *Stained Class* is riddled with backward messages – that is, if you spin the LP backwards, you'll hear passages you can't make out when the album is played normally. Perhaps most famously used on the intro to Deep Purple's 'Stormbringer' (where what appears to be a garbled snarl is actually David Coverdale growling a trail of obscenities which was then reversed) the prosecution failed to show why any sane person would want to spin an LP backwards anyway. But also, of course, the album included 'Beyond The Realms Of Death', a song which the prosecution held up as an obvious rallying cry for every heavy metal fan to finish themselves off.

Despite the fact that Belknap and Vance were young men with very troubled and dysfunctional backgrounds the case against both the band on trial and metal in general ground on, with an expert witness for the prosecution stating that both 'try suicide' and 'fuck the Lord' were easily discernible on the album. Even Roslaw Szaybo's iconic cover image of a laser beam passing through a head was held up as an example of how the band were advocating suicide. And whereas looking back now, this all looks like a desperate attempt to deflect attention away from Belknap's and Vance's difficult upbringing. It was also possibly a way to make a lot of money out of the band as Belknap's and Vance's parents were jointly looking for a cool $3 million from band and label. However, the moral crusade against metal in the US was particularly high at this time and the courtroom footage broadcast (and now available on the internet) shows not only the seriousness of the situation but also the stress that Halford, Tipton, Downing and Hill were under. One day they were musicians riding high on hard-fought and well-deserved success; the next they were in court, accused of blatantly bringing about the deaths of two young men through their music and potentially, had the civil action gone against them, then being further accused of aiding and abetting a suicide, or even murder. It's impossible to imagine how this must have affected the band members undergoing such an ordeal.

Halford, trying his own experiment, revealed that if you play the chorus of 'Exciter' backwards, it comes out something like: 'I-I-I asked her for a peppermint / I-I-I asked for her to get one.' 'We bought the album from a local supermarket,' Tipton told Al King twenty years later, 'played it backwards, normal speed, no editing. In 30 seconds we found "hey mom, my chair's broken" and "give me a peppermint" – in other words, phonetic flukes, harmless messages.' Unsurprisingly, after a gruelling four weeks, the judge eventually threw the whole case out.

Manager Bill Curbishley later famously (but rather tastelessly) was quoted as saying 'the only subliminal message I would put on an album would be "buy seven copies"'!

Painkiller (1990)

Personnel:
Rob Halford: lead vocals
Glenn Tipton: lead guitar
K.K. Downing: lead guitar
Ian Hill: bass guitar
Scott Travis: drums
Record label: CBS
Recorded at: Miraval Studios, France and Wisseloord, Studios, Holland, January to March 1990
Produced by: Chris Tsangarides & Judas Priest
Release date: 3 September 1990
Highest chart positions: UK: 26, US: 26
Running time: 46:08

> *By then they'd got the new drummer in, Scott Travis, who was leaps and bounds above any drummer they'd had up to that point bar, I suppose, Simon Phillips, who'd played on* Sin After Sin *but who'd come in as a session drummer* – Chris Tsangarides

Classic Rock magazine's April 2018 issue was largely given over to 'The Real 100 Greatest Albums Of The Nineties', which, depending on your read of choice, is always *Metallica* or *Nevermind*. But at No.25, sandwiched between Foo Fighters' *The Colour And The Shape* and the sole album from the short-lived collaboration between David Coverdale and Jimmy Page, came *Painkiller*, one of only three albums Judas Priest released that decade. Each album was given a short description, and Malcolm Dome offered this on the band's twelfth studio album:

> *Priest's output during the mid-to-late Eighties had suggested they were floundering and had been usurped by a new generation of metal heroes, so* Painkiller *was a crucial album for the band. And not just because they were revitalised. As they got heavier and tougher, taking elements from thrash and adapting them to their own style, Priest gave metal itself renewed impetus and set a template for what followed in the next decade. Tracks like 'Painkiller' and 'All Guns Blazing' symbolised the fact that the genre still had much to offer.*

By one of those odd quirks of fate, the magazine's rear cover carried a full-page advert for *Firepower*, the only Priest album since their 'reunification' to come close to replicating the hard-hitting stance of *Painkiller* itself.

Painkiller was the start of a period of major upheaval for Rob Halford, K.K. Downing, Glenn Tipton and Ian Hill. Once again they found themselves without a drummer, and they decided to work with a new producer, having had Tom Allom sat in the big leather chair for a decade. In the meantime, it would be hard to put from their minds the fact that in America legal proceedings were rumbling on in a case that could have massive implication for music in general and for the band members in particular. The result of all this uncertainty was that the band regrouped and came out with their most intense and visceral release ever. This might well have been a response to whatever was happening behind the scenes back in the States. But at the same time Halford was not only dissatisfied with the band in general but, looking around, was seeing the changes that metal was undergoing outside of the band's bubble and was immersing himself in it, soaking up new influences. 'During the *Painkiller* sessions, Rob kept going on about Pantera and how they sounded,' recalled Chris Tsangarides. 'I barely knew anything about them, they'd not broken big yet, and of course, they went on to be the support on the *Painkiller* tour. But I remember saying to Rob, "man, you're Judas Priest! What do you want to sound like someone else for? Because they all want to sound like you"!'

The renowned producer, who sadly died in January 2018 aged just 61, recalls that the band and one-time glorified studio tea boy had reconnected in the late Eighties:

> *They were playing in Japan, and I happened to be over there working on an album so I went off to see them and they couldn't have been more shocked and/or surprised and/or happy to see me pitch up in this place on the other side of the world. 'Why didn't you come to Hammersmith?' they asked me. Anyway, so we got back in touch with each other. A little later they were in the States watching MTV and this video comes on: 'bloody hell, that sounds really good; my God, the bass sound...' and they found out it was something I'd done, so they called me up and told me they were interested in doing an album together. So off I go to see them in Spain where they were living at the time, and Glenn played me some demos – well, when I say demos, it was the guitar riff and a drum machine, and this was 'Painkiller' – and I went, 'Woah, yeah, that's fab, I like that. But what are we going to do with it? Where are we going to find a drummer who can play that fast?' because it is as you know a ridiculous tempo. I hadn't heard anything like that since Anvil, I suppose, back in the early days, and even then that wasn't as fast as 'Painkiller'. 'Well, we've got one...' they said, and that turned out to be Scott.*

Mark Scott Travis apparently always lived for the day that he'd play for Judas Priest. One day his ex-Racer X bandmate and friend of Halford Jeff Martin told him that Priest had a vacant drum stool once more and the rest, as they say, is history. Tsangarides wanted to halt the slide in the band's fortunes and was probably the best man for the job. 'I always thought that if there was a weakness on *Sad Wings Of Destiny,* it was the drums, but it's of that era and the drums kind of suit the record. But it was a whole different ball game by the time they did *Painkiller*. And this was the first time in about three or four albums where they'd actually played together as a unit in the studio. Before then it was click tracks and drum machines, and samples and synthetic stuff. I just said, "no, I'd like you all to play together, given that we've got a proper drummer now."' He continued:

> *I think the fact that I really appreciate what they were doing, and they really appreciate what I do, shows in that I'm one of the very few people who has got a co-writing credit on their albums later on in life. 'A Touch Of Evil' on* Painkiller *is one I co-wrote, and there are a couple of songs after that on* Demolition, *'Metal Messiah' and 'Subterfuge' which are mine. I think that shows that we were always thinking along the same lines.*

Although inspired in choice of material and blessed with a contemporary cutting-edge sound *Painkiller* neither failed to halt the band's decline in fortunes nor convinced Halford that it was worth staying. It was a true return to form which unfortunately came a little too late. Despite a top honours review in *Kerrang!* which hailed it as 'a welcome return to form for these acknowledged masters of the genre' it failed to replicate even *Ram It Down*'s chart placing in the UK, although did marginally better in America. The UK saw a pair of singles lifted from the album, both of which met with no more than a modicum of success.

The cover art – not the band's best – was again supplied by Mark Wilkinson, and The Painkiller character – like The Hellion and The Metallian seemingly a lifetime ago – was given a few lines of descriptive backstory on the album's rear sleeve, or, more correctly, tray liner. This was the time of transition between formats and *Painkiller* was the band's first album to appear on CD and on LP, rather than on LP and CD, as sales of the 12" format slowly began to decline. It was finished in March 1990 but then left in limbo while waiting for legalities in America to finally come to a head. With the case dismissed on 24 August, the title track was released as a taster single for the album the following month. You're not going to convince me that 'Better By You, Better Than Me' was included on the 12" and CD single purely by coincidence, although whether it was to cash in on the infamy the song had unwittingly achieved or as a one-finger salute to the ridiculousness of the legal proceedings is open to conjecture.

'Painkiller' (Tipton / Halford / Downing)

You've been out of the public eye for some time. You want to make a statement. What do you do? You write a song like 'Painkiller', that's what. With its frenzied drum intro, hyperspeed riffing and furious vocals spat like bullets from the newly-shorn and almost demonic vocalist 'Painkiller' was the perfect way to shout out that the band were back on track. Unlike other trailer singles from the band like 'Living After Midnight' or 'Johnny B Goode', 'Painkiller' with its mind- and finger-bending solos, first from Tipton and then from Downing, and backed by a stunning video clip was designed to grab attention. It was also released in its full, unabashed, cranium-crunching, six-minute glory.

It's not a song you can ignore and, as with 'Exciter' and 'Rapid Fire', other album openers featuring a new drummer, 'Painkiller' allows Travis his share of the spotlight. As a single it was surely not expected to chart; flipped with 'United' and 'Better By You, Better Than Me' on the CD and 12" there wasn't much to tempt long-term fans, and it peaked at a lowly No.64. Its aim was simply to draw attention to itself and its parent album, and it did that spectacularly well. It's probably the most exciting and heaviest thing they'd written in a long, long time, and although the rest of the album struggled to match its magnificence, it was a hell of a good way to set things rolling.

'Hell Patrol' (Tipton / Halford / Downing)

Heavy and medium-paced, lyrically 'Hell Patrol' serves up an army of 'Nightriders, death dealers, storm bringers' who may be a battalion of the dead, or, more favourably, an allegory about the legions of metal fans the band often praised. Not a great song though, as it sort of canters along with only really the new boy behind the drums breaking a sweat.

The song also features the phrase 'and they'll paratamize you' although no-one knows what this is supposed to mean. Some suggestions have been that it's a made-up word based on paramatrize – to make you into a parameter – but there is urban slang to suggest it's a word for 'sodomise'. I prefer to think that it's Halford's second contribution to the ever-growing English dictionary.

'All Guns Blazing' (Tipton / Halford / Downing)

Opening with Halford singing solo before the band crash in all riffin' and smokin' 'All Guns Blazing' is pretty standard fare for the band, a chuggalong little number enlivened by Tipton delivering a solo that doesn't sound a million miles from his work on the title track. It made the cut live, and onstage proved itself to be quite a heavy little beast, but on the album, it's not only rather repetitive but also does call 'Painkiller' to mind – and that song's only just finished a few minutes back!

'Leather Rebel' (Tipton / Halford / Downing)

Not an ode to the metal community, 'Leather Rebel' is another of Halford's living off the grid characters, a bit like 'Running Wild', set to a fast backbeat and a riff of steel. The opening gives the game away. This song is going to be no slouch, and although the chorus is a bit on the wussy side it's a lively little blighter which scorches up the highway and wastes not a second of its three-and-a-half minute running time, the shortest actual song on the album. Downing adds some runs to the end as the song crashes to its conclusion.

'Metal Meltdown' (Tipton / Halford / Downing)

The guitarists split the intro here (in alphabetical order) as 'Metal Meltdown' (like 'Heavy Metal' a couple of years back) opens with a flurry of notes to set the mood and point out that this is indeed a Metal Song. Halford uses the majority of his range to great effect across the song which then gives way to a good, old fashioned Downing / Tipton / Downing / Tipton solo as Travis pounds away and Hill keeps things as steady as they can be.

The only reservation is that as the first side of the album closes you realise that, actually, you've heard a lot of this before. It's well played, yes, it's exciting, certainly, but there's not a lot new on offer.

'Night Crawler' (Tipton / Halford / Downing)

'Beware the beast in black...', eh? 'Night Crawler' is a fairly typical but lengthy (5:44) Priest outing with an atmospheric, moody, dry-ice laden intro which gives way to an enticing riff, some horror-based lyrics and a harmony solo – the likes of which you might think Downing actually envisioned so many years ago back in Gull's offices – from him and his opposite number. The spoken word passage is slightly irrelevant (the fact that it was edited completely out of the single and not even missed speaks volumes) but overall it's a song with a lot to commend it.

Technically you can call 'Night Crawler' the third single to be released from *Painkiller*, as a limited edition version appeared in April 1993 to promote the same month's Metal Works '73-'93 compilation release. Backed by 'Living After Midnight' with the red vinyl 12" and picture CD single both adding 'Breaking The Law', both unimaginatively drawn from *Priest... Live!*, it spent one week in the charts at No. 63.

'Between The Hammer & The Anvil' (Tipton / Halford / Downing)

A nice, moody intro with an underpinning drum pattern gives way to an explosive scream (and explosion), after which it's a heads-down riffer with an off-beat middle-eight and hammer, and anvil effects before Downing and then Tipton take centre stage. It's a strong offering which also features the producer's guitar work, and which ends with a nice slide into the album's second real highlight, 'A Touch Of Evil'.

'A Touch Of Evil' (Tipton / Halford / Downing / Tsangarides)

With an uncredited Don Airey on keyboards but a songwriting credit for producer Tsangarides (who'd originally had a rough tape of the song's bare-bones which Priest's songwriters took away and ran with) 'A Touch Of Evil' was the album's second single, released in March 1991 in time for the UK tour. The sleeve even carries the UK tour dates, although someone messed up and omitted the Belfast show from the list as if they'd forgotten that Northern Ireland is part of the United Kingdom.

The single was heavily edited, taking its running time down from 5:42 to 4:12, but wasn't really chart fodder anyway and spent just one week in the charts at No.58. 'Between The Hammer & The Anvil' appeared on the B-side, along with (on the 12" and CD) the chugga-chugga-chugga of 'You've Got

Another Thing Comin'' from *Priest... Live!*. In addition, there was the 'Access All Areas' picture disc, the CD came with a free patch and the 12" carried a 'Giant 60 x 40 *Painkiller* Poster' – surely a must for every household.

As an album track, though, 'A Touch Of Evil' is as moody and magnificent as Priest get, and after the title track is *Painkiller*'s second (and, in my opinion, only other real) highpoint. If 'Painkiller' is the cake, then 'A Touch Of Evil' is the icing. It's a cleverly constructed composition brimming with power and passion and follows a similar vein as 'Love Bites' where the atmosphere creates the moment and raises the hairs on the back of your neck. It's a song about desire and losing control to it, and if Halford's plaintive delivery after the solo and ensuing scream of 'you're possessing me' doesn't get to you, then check you've got a pulse.

'Battle Hymn' (Tipton / Halford / Downing)

Just shy of a minute's worth of pointless guitar instrumental to set things up for...

'One Shot At Glory' (Tipton / Halford / Downing)

Painkiller runs off with this bit of a damp squib, a ponderous rocker to which you can shake your head but do little else. Lyrically, it's about victory so could be taken as a nod to the court case, the enduring legacy of the band or Halford's decision to leave which, as mentioned earlier, was no great secret within the band. The soloing saves it from being a complete washout, although it's a shame the song didn't move in a different direction at that point rather than plunging back into the main riff. A little like the previous album's 'Monsters Of Rock' 'One Shot At Glory' is a bit something and nothing really, and ends the album rather disappointingly.

Post Album Events

After nearly two years off the road, Judas Priest re-appeared at the Concrete Foundations Forum, a showcase event held annually in Los Angeles, on 13 September 1990, where their set included two new songs 'Between The Hammer & The Anvil' and 'Leather Rebel'. The show was taped and 'Leather Rebel' was released as a bonus track to the 2001 re-issue of its parent album while 'Better By You, Better Than Me' (a surprising and, let's be fair, rather controversial addition to the setlist) was added to *Stained Class*. The tour proper commenced on 18 October in Montreal and kept them on the far side of the Atlantic until their Christmas break on 23 December. More Stateside dates opened the 1991 leg on 9 January (in Portland, Maine), followed by a quick flight to Brazil for Rock In Rio II on 23 January, before another flight brought them to Europe where things kicked off at the KB Hallen in Copenhagen on 31 Jan. By this time 'All Guns Blazing', 'Night Crawler' and 'Painkiller' were safely ensconced in the live show, 'A Touch Of Evil' also being played in the States but then discarded somewhere over the Atlantic.

The fairly lengthy European trek came to a close on 31 March in Dublin, following nine UK dates supported by Annihilator (the previous package which had also featured Pantera had now been slimmed down). Perhaps the most surprising thing about the whole tour was that, after opening with 'Hell Bent For Leather' and 'Grinder', the lights then dimmed for 'The Hellion' intro tape and 'Electric Eye': an odd place for it to fall in terms of pacing. The shows also featured a full-on drum solo, perhaps an indication that, as Chris Tsangarides said, the band did now have a skins-beater who was 'leaps and bounds' above many previous drummers, and also it gave the other members a much-welcomed breather.

From Eire, they stopped off in Alaska for three shows before continuing their journey to greet the ever-loyal Japanese fans with four shows to wrap up the tour. That should have been it, but then they were enrolled on the *Operation Rock 'N' Roll* package alongside Alice Cooper, Motörhead, Dangerous Toys and Metal Church. The times they were a-changing though; the metal circus crossed the US (with two final dates in Canada) through July and August to venues that were no longer as full as such a bill might expect as grunge was beginning to make its presence felt across the continent. Downing called it 'a tour I never wanted to do' given that they'd already toured *Painkiller* for almost a year and were feeling frazzled, but that 'despite the old issues [within the band] and us being burned out, we did Operation Rock 'N' Roll anyway and it really wasn't great...'

In answer to the question 'what direction will the new album go in?' in an interview in Metal Hammer during the European dates, Tipton responded:

> *Well, the kids liked* Painkiller, *so it will probably be in the same direction. But we never write on the road anyway. We won't think about the next album until we've finished touring. We'll have a break, and then it will be time to write. We are just enjoying touring at the moment.*

But as history shows, the next album would be a long way off. When Halford memorably screamed in 'Night Crawler' 'the end is drawing near' he wasn't wrong. He played his last show with Judas Priest on 19 August 1991 at Maple Leaf Gardens in Toronto. To fans it was a memorable show because (a) it was the last gig of the *Operation Rock 'N' Roll* extravaganza, and (b) due to a technical cock-up the stage set stairway which should have been raised to allow the singer to ride his Harley onstage was only part-way up when Halford appeared through the dry ice. He came out from underneath the riser and hit the bottom rung of the stairway. Fortunately, despite the collision and tumbling back off the bike, the only permanent damage was a broken nose which Halford never had fixed, claiming that every time he scratches it 'it's a permanent reminder.' For the reviewers, it was an easy pun that 'Painkiller' that night referred more to the paracetamol the singer was knocking back than the band's six-minute title-track thrashathon. However, two years later, again at the Concrete Foundations Forum in September 1993, Halford's new band Fight – originally seen as a side project but now a band in its own right – unveiled their debut album. It had been a good ride and had taken the band around the world numerous times, but the glory days of Judas Priest were seemingly over.

Epitaph?

Judas Priest released just three new albums in the Nineties, following *Painkiller* with *Jugulator* in 1997 and *'98 Live Meltdown* the following year. Earlier in their career, they would have achieved this in three years, or even less.

Rob Halford had announced his intention to pursue solo projects within Priest in March 1992 but officially left two months later. Onstage appearances with Pantera, Skid Row and Black Sabbath kept him in the spotlight and in September 1993, Fight – a band which allowed him to satiate his Pantera fixation and which also featured Scott Travis– unveiled their debut album, *War Of Words,* at the Concrete Foundations Forum at the Burbank Hilton, California. Following an EP *Mutations* and a second album, *A Small Deadly Space,* Fight had run its course and in February 1998 came the release of *Voyeurs*, an album recorded with Trent Reznor of Nine Inch Nails under the name Two. It's 'interesting'; let's leave it at that. Seemingly floundering for direction, the singer put together the self-referential Halford who released *Resurrection* in August 2000 and *Crucible* in June 2002 (as well as a live album *Live Insurrection* in 2001), the band following a more traditional heavy metal path and being all the better for doing so.

Meanwhile, Judas Priest seemed to disappear off the radar. *The Metal Works '73-'93* compilation, curated by K.K. Downing to keep things ticking over – apparently he'd wanted to amass a collection of their fastest material and call it Burning Sermons, but the Suits said no – appeared in May 1993. Meanwhile, Glenn Tipton locked himself away and came up with a solo album *Baptizm Of Fire* which features contributions from the likes of Cozy Powell, John Entwistle and Rob Trujillo and which finally reached the shops in February 1997. To be honest, it wasn't really worth the wait.

Finally, in May 1996 the band announced the recruitment of Tim 'Ripper' Owens from Ohio-based tribute band British Steel. The union – which also saw the return of Scott Travis to the Judas Priest drumstool – was blessed with the aforementioned *Jugulator* and ensuing live album, both of which are rather patchy. This was followed by the much more focused *Demolition* in July 2001 and *Live in London* (recorded at the Brixton Academy 19 December 2001) and released on DVD in July 2002 with a double CD featuring the full night's entertainment following in January 2003. Along the way, the band members watched as ex-drummer Dave Holland was charged and then imprisoned in 2004 for sexual abuse and attempted rape of a seventeen-year-old boy. As mentioned earlier, Holland passed away on 16 January 2018. They were somewhat amazed to be the inspiration behind the 2001 Mark Wahlberg / Jennifer Aniston film *Rock Star* in which the singer of a tribute band to fictional metallers Steel Dragon eventually replaces the singer of the band he idolises. 'I saw the movie and laughed all the way through it,' Tipton told Geoff Barton in *Classic Rock*. 'They actually asked us to write music for it, but we saw some of the roughs and decided to avoid it like the plague. It's a terrible case of Hollywood taking a very good idea – someone going from a cover band to the real thing – and just coming up with a load of nonsense.' And, of course,, Halford blew the cover on the worst-kept secret in metaldom in 1998 by revealing he was gay. 'I'm glad I did it then,' he later told *Classic Rock*, 'so that when I came back to Judas Priest it's all, you know, water under the bridge… If I'd stayed in the band I still wouldn't have come out… I wouldn't do anything to damage the Priest cause.'

The Halford-era albums were re-issued in 2001. Each studio album came with an unreleased studio song and live track, and the live albums both had a handful of rare or unreleased live cuts, but they were badly researched and could have been much better if designed by fans rather than Suits. But hey, buy them all and get a free box to put them in, along with a limited edition ten-track sampler of songs you've already got. *Metalogy* – a four CD / one DVD retrospective in a studded cardboard box – followed in 2004, and is currently listed in the *2018 Record Collector Rare Record Price Guide* as the most valuable item in the Judas Priest catalogue. The *Complete Albums Collection* presented all the albums including *Rocka Rolla* and *Sad Wings Of Destiny* (the first time these had really been referenced by the band in such a collection) in slipcases housed in one scrappy and poorly made cardboard box, was released in 2013. All the albums that is, aside from the four which featured Ripper Owens at the mike stand, which were left to languish in obscurity.

The inevitable return of Rob Halford was announced in July 2003. As Tipton recalled it to Geoff Barton: 'We made the decision very spontaneously one afternoon. We had a meeting to talk about the *Metalogy* box set with Rob at his house. We had no intention of talking about a reunion, but by the end of the afternoon, we'd decided to get back together. It was that simple.' Downing's autobiography tells a different story, suggesting that Sharon Osbourne offered them a shedload of cash to play the 2003 *Ozzfest* tour, so long as Halford was in the band, and so could substitute for Ozzy and front Sabbath if the Sabbath frontman's health required it. Halford had fronted Sabbath before, back when Ronnie James Dio had left, and, indeed, he would be called upon to do it again during the *Ozzfest* dates. Downing further stated that his fellow guitarist hadn't been happy with the suggestion of Halford returning. 'From the start, Glenn wasn't having any of it. I don't know why not.'

As for Ripper Owens, who'd done so much to keep the band from languishing in obscurity, according to whose account you believe he was dumped either by email or by fax.

Since the reformation, four more studio albums, *Angel Of Retribution* (2005), the misunderstood *Nostradamus* (2008), *Redeemer Of Souls* (2014) and the critically-acclaimed *Firepower* – seemingly everyone's favourite album of 2018 – have been added to the band's catalogue, alongside a plethora of live audio and visual recordings. But there was a further twist in the tale. With things seemingly going so well on the eve of a vague farewell tour that could have stretched on forever,Downing, the man who once famously declared 'I started Judas Priest with myself on guitar, Ian and another singer, Allan Atkins' suddenly quit the band for good. He announced on 20 April 2011 that 'there had been an ongoing breakdown in working relationships between myself, elements of the band and management for some time.' His departure left his former Freight bandmate as the sole remnant of the band's early (but not earliest) days. Downing was replaced by Richie Faulkner, a Londoner and member of the likes of Voodoo Six and more famously Lauren Harris's band, the singer once described as 'easy on the eye and painful on the ear' and, ironically, the daughter of Steve Harris from Iron Maiden, whose first real big break came when they supported Judas Priest over thirty years previously on the *British Steel* tour. Faulkner's first performance was on 25 May 2011, where the band (to add to the seeming incongruity of the situation) guested on talent/game show American Idol and romped through 'Living After Midnight' and 'Breaking The Law' as support to contestant James Durbin (who eventually finished fourth). And although the blond, Flying V wielding guitarist, was at first thought of as no more than a K.K. clone brought in to play second fiddle, Faulkner has become an integral part of the band, a precision soloist in his own right who's been given the chance to shine on every stage he's set foot on.

His partnership with Tipton was to be relatively short-lived though, as in February 2018 Tipton announced he would be retiring from live performances, having been diagnosed with Parkinson's Disease. At this point in time, he still guests with the band on a handful of numbers when health permits, but is unable to carry off anything like a full show.

Whatever the future may hold, Judas Priest will always be the quintessential traditional heavy metal band, and no account of the genre will ever be written without acknowledging their contribution to it. 'One life,' they famously sang, 'I'm going to live it up.' And they did.

Long live the Metal Gods!

Appendix One – Priest Re-Released: The Later Re-Issues

Like any band, Judas Priest's back catalogue has been widely exploited over the years. But in 2001 it was announced that the CBS (now Sony) albums would be remastered and re-issued, each with at least a pair of bonus tracks (one studio, one live was the original plan, but that plan eventually went out the window). The twelve CDs were issued in batches of four – with Back On Black making them available on vinyl – and if you picked up the second set (*Sin After Sin – Unleashed In The East*) altogether they came in a natty collectors' box. You could also collect a ten-track promotional CD which featured six standard album cuts, two from the Japanese *Live And Rare* CD ('Beyond the Realms Of Death', the Agora Ballroom live cut, and 'Private Property' from Kiel Auditorium, St Louis, 1986) and two CD-Rom tracks ('Turbo Lover' and 'You've Got Another Thing Comin'') from the *Priest…Live* VHS cassette – this didn't appear on DVD until 2003, as part of the *Electric Eye* package.

Unfortunately, the re-issues lacked any real detail, being thrown together by businessmen rather than fans, and there's rarely anything explicit in the booklet as to the provenance of the bonus material. In fairness, the first batch of four releases (*British Steel* to *Defenders Of The Faith*) did set out some basic details, but the former's live version of 'Grinder', listed in the booklet as being from the UK *British Steel* tour, opens with a rousing cry of 'Long Beach, California.' Someone should have done their homework: not only is it obvious from that opening shout, but any self-respecting fan of the band would tell you that on the UK *British Steel* tour, the band didn't actually play anything from *British Steel*!

A summary of the bonus material on those re-issues is given below:

Sin After Sin

'Race With The Devil' is an outtake from *Stained Class* sessions and is a pretty straightforward but very interesting take on Gun's 1967 shuffle. The live version of 'Jawbreaker' is one of several songs taken from the gig at Long Beach, California, 5 May 1984.

Stained Class

A (fairly obvious) left-over from the *Ram It Down* sessions, credited just to Tipton and Halford, 'Fire Burns Below' is an interesting number, and very much of its time with an Eighties' sound and drum machine pounding away in the background. It should have been worked on and given space on the album, as it's a passionate and atmospheric little beast with a lot of interesting guitar work and, at nearly seven minutes long, would have given *Ram It Down* some extra depth. 'Better By You, Better Than Me' was taken from the band's appearance at the Concrete Foundations Forum, Los Angeles, 13 September 1990, at the very start of the *Painkiller* trek. If the whole set still exists, it would make an interesting live release, given the variety of material played on the night.

Killing Machine

Reworked to appear as 'Rock Hard Ride Free' on *Defenders Of The Faith* 'Fight For Your Life' is an outtake from the *Screaming For Vengeance* sessions and, as the later version shows, definitely needed some work. The electrifying 'Riding On The Wind' is taken from the US Festival, California, 29 May 1983, the show later re-issued as the bonus DVD with *Screaming For Vengeance – 30th Anniversary Edition* in 2012.

Unleashed In The East

The four bonus cuts here – 'Rock Forever', 'Delivering The Goods', 'Hell Bent For Leather' and 'Starbreaker' – are all from the Japanese album *Priest In The East*. 'Rock Forever' and 'Hell Bent For Leather' had appeared previously in the UK on the bonus single which came with the album and the short version of 'Delivering The Goods' was on the B-side of 'Living After Midnight'.

British Steel

Some things are best left locked away, and the awful 'Red, White & Blue', an outtake from the *Turbo* sessions, should never have been allowed to see daylight. This slab of leaden pseudo-patriotic drivel is truly horrendous. Please, make it stop... If you've managed not to rip the CD from your player and hurl the disc across the room, the live version of 'Grinder', as mentioned above from the Long Beach, California, show on 5 May 1984 is extremely good and makes up for the three-and-a-half minutes of torment you've just subjected yourself to. Almost.

Point Of Entry

As mentioned earlier, 'Thunder Road' is a good song in its own right but does sound at times, not unlike 'Johnny B. Goode' so presumably got the heave-ho from *Ram It Down* for that reason. It's a fast-paced song with a nifty time-change which, again, would not only have fitted well on its parent album, but would have given it some fire and been the ideal replacement for the turgid 'I'm A Rocker'. 'Desert Plains' is from an early date on the *Fuel For Life* tour, recorded at Kiel Auditorium, St Louis, Missouri 23 May 1986.

Screaming For Vengeance

'Prisoner Of Your Eyes' is one of the *Twin Turbo* casualties, and is – to be honest – a rather stilted ballad with little to redeem it aside from Halford's mournful delivery and, to be fair, a really good solo. It would have been the perfect lighter-in-the-air job, although as it's seven minutes long, it would also make the perfect toilet break. Halford dusted it down and re-recorded it with a bit more oomph as a bonus track on his self-titled band's 2001 live album *Live Insurrection*. The live version of 'Devil's Child' is drawn from the soundtrack to the *Judas Priest Live* video, originally released in 1983, and recorded at the Mid South Coliseum, Memphis, Tennessee, on 12 December 1982.

Defenders Of The Faith

Another ballad, another outtake from *Turbo* sessions, 'Turn On Your Light' is not something to get too excited about, although when everyone finally kicks in around the four-minute mark, the song does gear up considerably and bares its teeth until the fade a minute or so later. As such, it's not as bad as 'Red, White & Blue' – but then, not much is – but it's hard to see this ever being a serious contender unless the band had been able to release a sprawling and varied double album. Which, of course, they weren't! The live coupling of 'Heavy Duty' / 'Defenders Of The Faith' come from the good old Long Beach 1984 gig.

Turbo

Whether by luck or design 'All Fired Up' is a left-over actually married up with its parent album. It does veer into 'Freewheeling Burning' territory (which is no bad thing in itself) and could easily have replaced some of the crowd-pleasing fodder that eventually appeared on *Turbo* and upped the excitement somewhat. 'Locked In' is another from Kiel Auditorium in May 1986.

Priest...Live

The three live bonus tracks are all from (by now) familiar sources. 'Screaming For Vengeance' was recorded at the Mid South Coliseum, Memphis, Tennessee, on 12 December 1982; 'Rock Hard, Ride Free' is taken from Long Beach, California, 5 May 1984; and 'Hell Bent For Leather' from Kiel Auditorium, Saint Louis, Missouri, 23 May 1986.

Ram It Down

Unusually for a studio album *Ram It Down* came with two bonus live cuts: 'Night Comes Down' is from Long Beach 1984 again, while 'Bloodstone' is from the *Judas Priest Live* video (Memphis, Tennessee, 12 December 1982).

Painkiller

'Living Bad Dreams' is actually a very good, mid-paced song (with evidence of Don Airey's keyboards in the background) which failed to make the final cut for *Painkiller* – which is a shame as it's a very interesting, menacing, belligerent number, and certainly wouldn't have been out of place. Some great guitar work too. Should have been on the album, no question... The live track this time around is a rare outing for 'Leather Rebel', a second track taken from the Concrete Foundations Forum show on 13 September 1990.

In addition, in May 2004, not long after Halford had re-joined the band, came *Metalogy*, a four-CD plus DVD box set (the DVD being the Mid South Coliseum, Memphis, Tennessee, 12 December 1982 video getting a digital revamp). Amongst the 65 audio tracks were a handful of diamonds and nuggets: 'The Green Manalishi (With The Two-Pronged Crown)' came from the Palladium, NY, July 1981 show; 'Love Bites' from Kiel Auditorium, 23 May 1986; 'Hot Rockin'' from a 12" promo release, recorded in Chicago (presumably 8 May) 1981; 'The Hellion' / 'Electric Eye' again from a promo 12", recorded at San Antonio Civic Centre, 10 September 1982 (other tracks from this show appeared on the *Screaming For Vengeance – 30th Anniversary Edition*; and although 'Grinder' is credited to Long Beach California, May 1986, it's actually the Long Beach 1984 version, once again incorrectly listed. The other item of interest is 'Heart Of A Lion', another *Turbo* outtake again covered by Halford (the band) on *Live Insurrection* which, to be fair, isn't all that bad – a mid-paced slugger with a strong chorus sung in an unbelievably high register.

It's worth noting that the entire Long Beach, California, 5 May 1984 set was later issued as bonus material with *Defenders Of The Faith* – Special 30th Anniversary Edition in 2015, and the set from the Kiel Auditorium, Saint Louis, Missouri, two years later came (again split over two discs) with *Turbo 30* in 2017. The *Screaming For Vengeance* – 30th Anniversary Edition re-issue in 2012 carried a bonus DVD recorded at the US Festival in San Bernadino, California, on 29 May 1983, and with six bonus audio tracks. 'Electric Eye', 'Riding On The Wind', 'You've Got Another Thing Coming' and 'Screaming For Vengeance' are taken from a show at San Antonio Civic Centre, 10 September 1982; 'Devil's Child' (Mid South Coliseum, Memphis, Tennessee, 12 December 1982) and 'Prisoner Of Your Eyes' (*Turbo* outtake) are the tracks which graced the album's first revamp.

Appendix Two – The Video Clips

The release of *British Steel* pretty much coincided with the birth of the video age and, although MTV premiering with 'Video Killed The Radio Star' on 1 August 1981 was still a little way in the future, the record industry was beginning to cotton on to the advantages of the promotional video. True, they could be expensive to produce – although generally not in Priest's case – but there were a growing number of outlets on which videos could be aired and if nothing else it meant that a *Top Of The Pops* slot could still be accessed even if the artist was on tour abroad. Never again should the band mess up by putting a trip to London to mime like muppets ahead of a sell-out home crowd in Birmingham. Twice.

As a result, *British Steel* afforded their band their first two promotional video shoots, and the album's first single 'Living After Midnight' came complete with a clip of the band and their fans arriving, performing and, well, generally living after midnight – a fact made clear by the shot of a clock face, its hands staunchly erect, as the fans tumble onto their coach for the trip back home. It's cheesy, certainly, but effective all the same, especially the view from the audience of the band going through its paces on a relatively small stage.

From that early masterpiece Halford, Tipton and Downing seemed to throw themselves into whatever map cap idea video directors came up with, Hill and Holland generally observing events from the sidelines, which, given most of the storylines, was the best place to be. The band's second effort, 'Breaking The Law', has gone on to become a camp metal comedy classic. It's hard to know when to stop laughing. The angst-ridden Halford mimes the first verse in an open-top car en route to meeting up with the guitarists and robbing a bank, terrorising customers with their guitars and waking a sleeping security guard in the process. Once in the vault Halford bends the steel bars with his bare hands to make off not with a big bag of cash but with a gold disc for *British Steel*. The guard snatches a cardboard guitar, the band speed off, and the overriding message seems to be that (a) maybe crime does pay and (b) rock video directors are all completely deranged. But two minutes and thirty-six seconds in the company of the 'Breaking The Law' video is never time wasted.

From that fairly low bar, the band then went on to turn in generally low-budget rib-ticklers on a fairly regular basis. For 'Don't Go', the band are playing in a room, and they all go (despite the title), one at a time. Hill walks through the door at height and falls. Downing goes next and winds up in an endless corridor full of rabbits which gives way to another door behind which is a group of writhing women, pretty much an essential in an Eighties metal video, and certainly more essential than rabbits. Tipton pushes past Halford and becomes a Thirties mobster. Halford leaps around in a spacesuit and was apparently sick when flipping upside down. The video probably works as some kind of artistic statement about the fear of loss and rejection. Maybe.

For 'Heading Out To The Highway' the band perform in front of a terribly-painted endless desert road backdrop, cut against Halford starting a race between two cars driven by petrol heads Downing and Tipton while Hill and Holland look on. Both cars have *Point Of Entry* emblazoned across the windscreen, just in case you forget, and Halford really camps it up singing to the backing track as the cars line up at the starting line. Impossible not to like, and Hill should have been nominated for an Oscar when the camera pans to him and catches his intense concentration on the race unfolding before him. The final *Point Of Entry* clip is the funniest, as 'Hot Rockin'' sees the band working out in the gym, with Halford below the camera's eyeline and making a point of entry every time he completes a push-up. As if to counter the writhing women earlier, the band are all topless which might, or might not, make the video more appealing. Actually, it doesn't. Halford mugs to the camera, then drives to the set where the band go through their paces, rockin' so hot that the amps explode, fire spreads through the leads and the vocalist actually voluntarily sets fire to his boots, forgetting that no matter how much protection he might have on, his little pinkies would still get incredibly hot. And they did. The mic catches fire, the headstocks are all on fire, and Holland looks really natty in a leather jacket and tie, which somehow never really caught on with the rest of the band.

New album, bigger budget. Welcome to the noise pollution test zone (which looks like it might be Battersea power station) in which the band chug-chug-chug along to 'You've Got Another Thing Comin'' – on a sound stage featuring their new laser light show – while an anonymous bureaucrat makes his way towards them and whips out his equipment. The dB meter goes wild at the volume, and despite looking threateningly at the band with all the menace an anonymous bureaucrat can muster, his head explodes. Really. To be fair, the band are giving it all they've got with their performance, although without a mic Halford does really ham things up, and there's little real evidence of either Hill or Holland in the clip.

Next up, 'Freewheel Burning', probably needs little introduction, being cut from the same inane cloth as 'Breaking The Law'. There's this young whippersnapper playing an array of arcade video games interspersed with the band on form and again performing with their current full US stage show. Various clips of Halford are crudely superimposed onto the lad's screen, the stage lasers blast into reality, and thankfully Holland has ditched the tie. It's a marvellous piece of twaddle, especially the line of extras headbanging at their games, but once again the actual footage of the band is terrific. Back in the arcade the pressure mounts on our little munchkin as the song screws itself into a climax and then he slumps back in his seat, exhausted by the effort but probably thinking that was the best 10p he'd ever spent. The screen flashes up 'Warning: The Surgeon General Has Determined That Heavy Metal Is Dangerous To Your Health' and it's game over, boy. He probably should have been in school anyway.

Most fans would really prefer bands to ditch the silly storylines and just present a pseudo-live performance, which is what makes 'Love Bites' so appealing. With minimal faffing about 'Love Bites' shows to great effect the band miming on their Metallian stage set. Effective and exciting, the performance from all concerned is electrifying, and there's little camera mugging this time around. The brief clip of live footage to try to make it look like this is truly live, rather than a staged performance, is rather cheesy, but it's arguably the second best video Judas Priest have ever made. Which is more than can be said for the next pair.

In a post-apocalyptic society the band race motorbikes across a desert wasteland, seemingly followed by a roller-skating robotic creature with a skeletal head. And there are some foxy females, too – why wouldn't there be, in a post-apocalyptic wasteland? – with a terribly gratuitous shot of a woman wearing not a lot chasing off after a tyre as Tipton's solo despatches one of the skull-heads. And that's 'Turbo Lover' in a nutshell, really. This goes on for four or so minutes – the album track is edited – and as the band speed off Rob gets separated from the pack – 'no Rob, no: you're going the wrong way,' you might want to shout at the screen – and is pursued by old skully while the rest watch the chase through binoculars. Well, Downing and Tipton do anyway; the budget obviously couldn't stretch to four pairs, so Hill and Holland look vaguely bemused. As indeed they should. But there's more, as 'Locked In' continues where 'Turbo Lover' left off. The discombobulated vocalist is captured and then imprisoned by a tribe of primitive – but highly alluring, naturally – women and locked in (see what they did there?) to a cage where he swings upside down, barely able to conceal his laughter. Downing and Tipton come to the rescue while Hill and Holland look on. The skull-headed creatures look on too until the dynamic duo spring their frontman – although you could argue that anyone responsible for the lyrics to 'Rock You All Around The World' should really be left incarcerated anyway. Whereas the interplay between Halford and Downing is something that the Chuckle Brothers might have been proud of, the highlight of the on-screen action must be when Hill and Holland (yes, they've finally turned up) drop a rope ladder. The band speed off, presumably to do good elsewhere on the planet. Hoorah!

'Johnny B. Goode', shot at Roxy Club in Amsterdam on 3 April 1988, gets top marks for the black and white clip, bonus points for not including any excerpts from the deplorable movie, and no marks for the song itself. Downing really does give it some though, as do the stage divers – especially the bloke you see stage-diving at least four times. With slicked back hair and shades, Holland looks like he's there to collect a debt and certainly not someone you'd care to meet in an alleyway. A really good performance, although best watched with the sound turned off, and not a bad video, although it pales into insignificance when compared to 'Painkiller', the best video made by Judas Priest by a million miles. A grainy, black and white bomb blast of strobe-driven fast edits creates an electrifying, difficult to ignore, impossible to forget visual portrayal of Priest at their finest. Arresting, exhilarating, unmissable, and also vaguely disturbing, the 'Painkiller' video is a roller-coaster ride through Hell, and a clip every director should watch before commencing work with whatever metal band they're about to film ... Forget bank robbers dressed as priests or dummies with exploding heads, this is the way to project a band like Priest in the video era. Nothing tops this.

For the final Priest video of this era, 'A Touch Of Evil', things revert to type with a jumble of assorted gobbledygook. At the altar of censorship, cassettes are being shovelled into a fire while assorted circus characters, a snake and a fundamentalist preacher all put in an appearance in some kind of jumbled narrative with short bursts of the band mixed in. Presumably, the young lad is thought to be possessed to tie in with the lyrics, but it's all a bit of a hotchpotch of clichés really, although sadly lacking in rabbits. I've never lost any sleep over it, nor do I have the faintest idea what it's about, but, for what it's worth, the snake steals the show.

Appendix Three – Bibliography

The following books should be at home in any fan's collection:

Atkins, A. & Daniels, N., *Dawn Of The Metal Gods – My Life In Judas Priest And Heavy Metal* (Iron Pages, 2009; ISBN 9783931624569)
Daniels, N., *The Story Of Judas Priest – Defenders Of The Faith* (Omnibus Press, 2007; ISBN 9781846096907)
Daniels, N., *British Steel* (Wymer Publishing, 2011; ISBN 9780955754265)
Downing, K.K., *Heavy Duty – Days And Nights In Judas Priest* (Constable, 2018; ISBN 9781472128706)
Gett, S., *Heavy Duty* (Cherry Lane Books, 1984; ISBN 0711905975)
Popoff, M., *Heavy Metal Painkillers* (ECW Press, 2007; ISBN 9871550227840)

Other Books, Magazines And Newspapers Referenced

Tatler, B. with Tucker, J., *Am I Evil? The Music, The Myths And Metallica* by (Self-published, ISBN 987-0-9564034-0-7)
Carlos Clarke, B., *Shooting Sex – The Definitive Guide To Undressing Beautiful Strangers* by (Self-published, ISBN 0-95434-620-3)
'Rocking The Night Away' by Robin Smith, *Reading Evening Post* cover date 23 August 1975
'Info Riot' by Barry Lazell, *Sounds* cover date 14 July, 4 August and 15 September 1984. 'Info Riot' was an information exchange in which someone – in this case Paul Stock, of Grays, Essex – would write in and ask for a band discography and Barry Lazell would oblige. Then other fans would follow this up and contribute more detail to be published in later weeks. It was funny to see that I was one of the contributors, as was *Forearm Smash* and later *Kerrang!* writer Paul Miller (R.I.P.).
'Boom! Pow! Blam! Whack! Slam! Crash! (Or – Look out, Barton's gone bananas over the new Judas Priest album)' review of *Sin After Sin* by Geoff Barton, *Sounds* cover date 30 April 1977
'Screaming For Vengeance' by Dave Ling, *Classic Rock Presents Heavy Metal* (2007)
'The Real 100 Greatest Albums Of The 60s', *Classic Rock* issue 259, March 2019, in which various reviewers tackled the mammoth chart. Spooky Tooth's *Spooky Two* (on which 'Better By You, Better Than Me' appeared) clocked in at No.62
'Ian Burden And The Human League' by Ian Harrison, *Mojo* issue 296, July 2018
'As Butch As A Bubble Bath' review of *Killing Machine* by Pete Silverton, *Sounds* 28 October 1978
'Preaching violence…' review of *Unleashed In The East* by Steve Gett, *Melody Maker* cover date 15 September 1979
'It's cataclysmic… It's blistering… It's… Apocalypse now' review of *Unleashed In The East* by Geoff Barton, *Sounds* cover date unknown
'The Buyers' Guide… Judas Priest' by Nick Ruskell, *Planet Rock* issue 5,

January 2018
'Light Up The Sky' review of Judas Priest and Iron Maiden at Hammersmith Odeon, *Sounds* cover date 22 March 1980 [When I photocopied this many years ago the bottom corner of the page was turned, and I can't work out who the reviewer was. Sorry!]
'British Rubble', interview with Glenn Tipton by Geoff Barton and Ross Halfin, *Sounds* cover date 26 April 1980
'Metallic K.O.', Monsters Of Rock review by Allan Jones, *Melody Maker* cover date 23 August 1980
'Storming The Castle', Monsters Of Rock review by Geoff Barton and Robbi Millar, *Sounds* cover date 23 August 1980
'Storming The Castle', Monsters Of Rock review by Mike Nicholls, *Record Mirror* cover date 23 August 1980
'Roaches And Lingerie' by Geoff Barton, *Sounds* cover date 8 August 1981
'Monolithic Murder' review of *Point of Entry* by Geoff Barton, *Sounds* cover date 7 March 1981
'Judas Priest' by Steve Gett, *Kerrang!* issue 20 cover date 15-28 July 1982
'Scream And Scream Again' review of *Screaming For Vengeance* by Steve Gett, *Kerrang!* issue 19 cover date 1–15 July 1982
'Vengeance Is Mine' – *Screaming For Vengeance* album review by Philip Bell, *Sounds* cover date 3 July 1982
'Take These Chains' [sic] single review, author unknown, *Sounds* cover date 23 October 1982
'The Making Of *Screaming For Vengeance*' by Xavier Russell, Rock Candy issue 6, Feb-March 2018
'The Number Of The Priest' by Philip Bell, *Sounds* cover date 7 August 1982
'Metal Daze' review of the US Festival by Laura Canyon, *Kerrang !* issue 46, cover date 14-27 July 1983
'Chain Reaction!' by Dave Dickson, *Kerrang!* issue 59, cover date 12-25 January 1984
'Weekend Warriors: Overkill, Over There' review of Dortmund Festival by Howard Johnson, *Kerrang!* issue 59, cover date 12-25 January 1984
Review of Hammersmith Odeon show by Mick Wall, *Kerrang!* issue 59, cover date 12-25 January 1984
'Self Defence' by Steve Gett, *Sounds*, cover date 17 December 1983
Defenders Of The Faith album review by Howard Johnson, *Kerrang!* issue 60, cover date 26 January-8 February
'Faith Healers' review of *Defenders Of The Faith* by Geoff Barton, *Sounds*, cover date 7 January 1984
Review of *Turbo* by Dave Dickson, *Kerrang!* issue 117, cover date 3-16 April 1986
Review of *Turbo* by Garry Sharpe, *Metal Forces* issue 17
Review of 'Turbo Lover' by Dave Dickson, *Kerrang!* issue 119, cover date 1-14 May 1986
Review of Los Angeles show by Derek Oliver, *Kerrang!* issue 124, cover date 10-23 July 1986

Review of Judas Priest at Hammersmith Odeon by Paul Miller, *Kerrang!* issue 194, cover date 2 July 1988
'Fall To Your Knees And Repent, If You Please' by Al King, *Classic Rock* issue 160, June 2011
'The Real 100 Greatest Albums Of The Nineties' by Malcolm Dome, *Classic Rock* issue 247, April 2018
'Say It Again, Glenn' by Martin Groß, *Metal Hammer* vol.6 issue 6, cover date 11-24 March 1991
'Recall For The Priest' by Geoff Barton, *Classic Rock* issue 74, Christmas 2004
All chart information is taken from *The Complete Book Of British Charts* by Neil Warwick, Jon Kutner and Tony Brown (Omnibus Press ISBN 1-844449-058-0) and *The Great Metal Discography* by M.C. Strong (Mojo Books, ISBN1-84195-185-4)

Also from Sonicbond Publishing

On Track series

Queen Andrew Wild 978-1-78952-003-3

Emerson Lake and Palmer Mike Goode 978-1-78952-000-2

Deep Purple and Rainbow 1968-79 Steve Pilkington 978-1-78952-002-6

Yes Stephen Lambe 978-1-78952-001-9

Blue Oyster Cult Jacob Holm-Lupo 978-1-78952-007-1

The Beatles Andrew Wild 978-1-78952-009-5

Roy Wood and the Move James R Turner 978-1-78952-008-8

Genesis Stuart MacFarlane 978-1-78952-005-7

Jethro Tull Jordan Blum 978-1-78952-016-3

The Rolling Stones 1963-80 Steve Pilkington 978-1-78952-017-0

Judas Priest John Tucker 978-1-78952-018-7

Toto Jacob Holm-Lupo 978-1-78952-019-4

Van Der Graaf Generator Dan Coffey 978-1-78952-031-6

Frank Zappa 1966 to 1979 Eric Benac 978-1-78952-033-0

Elton John in the 1970s Peter Kearns 978-1-78952-034-7

The Moody Blues Geoffrey Feakes 978-1-78952-042-2

The Beatles Solo 1969-1980 Andrew Wild 978-1-78952-042-2

Steely Dan Jez Rowden 978-1-78952-043-9

On Screen series

Carry On... Stephen Lambe 978-1-78952-004-0

Audrey Hepburn Ellen Cheshire 978-1-78952-011-8

Powell and Pressburger Sam Proctor 978-1-78952-013-2

Seinfeld Seasons 1 to 5 Stephen Lambe 978-1-78952-012-5

Francis Ford Coppola Stephen Lambe 978-1-78952-022-4

Other Books

Not As Good As The Book Andy Tillison 978-1-78952-021-7

The Voice. Frank Sinatra in the 1940s

Stephen Lambe 978-1-78952-032-3

and many more to come!